# BLACK BOOK ORDER FORM

Send _____ copies of the
**Super Deluxe Corvette Black Book 1953-1987**

| | |
|---|---|
| @ 9.95 each $_____ . _____ | |
| Ohio residents add .55 sales tax _____ . _____ | |
| Postage/handling | $2.00 |
| **Check/money order enclosed** $_____ . _____ | |

Name _____

Street _____

City _____ State _____ Zip _____

Mail Order To: **Michael Bruce Associates, Inc.**
Post Office Box 396
Powell, Ohio 43065

---

# BLACK BOOK ORDER FORM

Send _____ copies of the
**Super Deluxe Corvette Black Book 1953-1987**

| | |
|---|---|
| @ 9.95 each $_____ . _____ | |
| Ohio residents add .55 sales tax _____ . _____ | |
| Postage/handling | $2.00 |
| **Check/money order enclosed** $_____ . _____ | |

Name _____

Street _____

City _____ State _____ Zip _____

Mail Order To: **Michael Bruce Associates, Inc.**
Post Office Box 396
Powell, Ohio 43065

# BLACK BOOK
# ORDER FORM

# BLACK BOOK
# ORDER FORM

# The Corvette Black Book

Super Deluxe Edition 1953-1987

Published By
Michael Bruce Associates, Inc.
Post Office Box 396
Powell, Ohio 43065

## Contents

| | | | | | |
|---|---|---|---|---|---|
| Glossary | 4 | | | 1975 Corvette | 54 |
| Statistics | 5 | 1963 Corvette | 30 | 1976 Corvette | 56 |
| Instructions | 6 | 1964 Corvette | 32 | 1977 Corvette | 58 |
| 1953 Corvette | 10 | 1965 Corvette | 34 | 1978 Corvette | 60 |
| 1954 Corvette | 12 | 1966 Corvette | 36 | 1979 Corvette | 62 |
| 1955 Corvette | 14 | 1967 Corvette | 38 | 1980 Corvette | 64 |
| 1956 Corvette | 16 | 1968 Corvette | 40 | 1981 Corvette | 66 |
| 1957 Corvette | 18 | 1969 Corvette | 42 | 1982 Corvette | 68 |
| 1958 Corvette | 20 | 1970 Corvette | 44 | 1984 Corvette | 70 |
| 1959 Corvette | 22 | 1971 Corvette | 46 | 1985 Corvette | 72 |
| 1960 Corvette | 24 | 1972 Corvette | 48 | 1986 Corvette | 74 |
| 1961 Corvette | 26 | 1973 Corvette | 50 | 1987 Corvette | 76 |
| 1962 Corvette | 28 | 1974 Corvette | 52 | Illustrations | 78 |

Michael Bruce Associates, Inc. acknowledges with appreciation the following Corvette enthusiasts who contributed their technical expertise to this publication: Noland Adams, Dan Aldridge, John Amgwert, Pat Baker, Dave Burroughs, M. F. Dobbins, Sam Folz, Mike Hunt, Paul Kitchen, Jim Krughoff, Gary Lisk, Bill Locke, Bob McDorman, Chip Miller, Bill Mock, Jeff Painter, Bill Rhodes, Lou Vitalle, Jerry Wadsworth and Don Williams. Special thanks also to the Chevrolet Motor Division of General Motors.

**Notice:** The Corvette Black Book and its publisher, Michael Bruce Associates, Inc. have no relationship or connection whatever with Hearst Business Media Corporation, its parent or affiliated corporations, or the Black Book published by National Auto Research Division of Hearst Business Media Corporation.

**Cover:** Photo and design by Mike Antonick. Corvette owned by Bill Munzer.

10-9-8-7

ISBN: 0-933534-17-5

BOOK TRADE DISTRIBUTION BY:

*Motorbooks International*
Publishers & Wholesalers Inc.
Osceola, Wisconsin 54020, USA ®

# GLOSSARY

**Big block:** V-8 engines of 396, 427 and 454-cubic-inch displacement.

**Big tank:** Optional 36 gal. gas tank for 1963-67; 24 gal. for 1961-62.

**Blue Flame:** Six cylinder engine of 1953, 1954 and a few 1955 models.

**Body off:** Restoration in which body was removed from the frame.

**Bolt on:** 1967 optional cast aluminum wheel.

**Bucket:** Headlight container for 1953-1955, and 1963-present models.

**Bullet:** Individual air cleaners of 1953 and early 1954.

**Buzzer:** The tachometer warning device used briefly in 1963, or the speedometer warning device optional in 1967-1969.

**Casting number:** Usually refers to the number cast into the block, but could refer to other cast numbers on engine and other components.

**Classic:** 1953-1962 Corvette.

**Collector Edition:** Specially equipped and trimmed 1982 model.

**Convertible:** Soft top Corvettes built between 1956-1975.

**Corvette Black Book:** Pocket "bible" of Corvette facts.

**Coupe:** 1963-1967 fixed top Corvette. T-top models built between 1968-1975 are sometimes also called coupes.

**Doghouse:** Fuel injection plenum chamber.

**Drum brake:** All Corvettes built before 1965 have them, but the term usually refers to the few 1965 models without discs.

**Fuelie:** 1957-1965 fuel injected Corvette. (Not cross fire injection.)

**Gold line:** Optional 1965-1966 gold stripe tire.

**Gymkhana:** Optional suspension package.

**Headrest:** Optional headrests for 1966-1968 models.

**Knock-off:** 1963-1966 optional cast aluminum wheel. Evidence suggests 1963 was over-the-counter only.

**Late model:** 1968-1982 Corvette.

**Mid year:** 1963-1967 Corvette.

**NCCC:** National Council of Corvette Clubs

**NCRS:** National Corvette Restorers Society

**NOS:** New Old Stock (brand new old parts).

**Numbers match:** Stamped and cast codes indicate original parts.

**Pace Car:** Limited edition replica of the 1978 Indianapolis 500 pace car.

**Prefix:** Alpha stamping into engine identifying engine build plant. Followed by code indicating date of final assembly.

**Red line:** Optional 1967-1969 red stripe tire.

**Roadster:** 1953-1955 Corvette.

**RPO:** Regular Production Option/Order.

**Side pipes:** Optional 1965-67, 1969 side mount exhausts.

**Silver Anniversary:** Two tone silver 1978 paint option.

**Small block:** V-8 engines of 265, 283, 305 (1980 California only), 327 and 350-cubic-inch displacement.

**Solid axle:** 1953-1962 Corvette.

**Split window:** 1963 Corvette coupe.

**Sticker:** Price posted on government required window sticker; retail.

**Sting Ray:** 1963-1967 Corvette.

**Stingray:** 1969-1976 Corvette.

**Suffix:** Alpha stamping into engine which identifies engine type.

**T-top:** 1968-1982 Corvette with removable roof panels.

**Teak:** Teakwood steering wheel optional in 1965-1966.

**Tele:** Optional telescopic steering column.

**VIN:** Vehicle Identification Number; serial number.

# STATISTICS

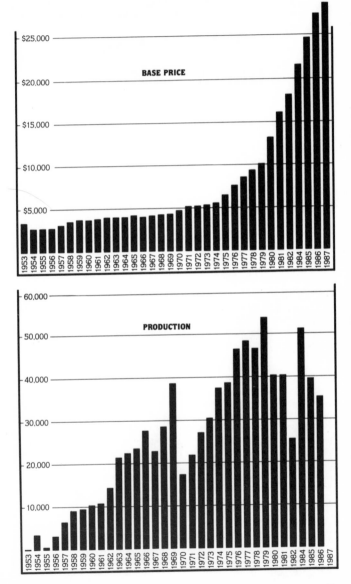

# HOW TO USE
# THIS INFORMATION

As most automobiles. Corvettes are laden with a plethora of number designations. Some numbers are insignificant. but others can be important in determining a Corvette's authenticity. Here's what to check.

## Body/Chassis Number

The most familiar number is the **body/chassis number**, also referred to as the **serial number**, or **vehicle identification number**. It is this number which appears on most auto titles, though some states have used others such as engine numbers.

The **body/chassis** number is assigned during vehicle assembly. Each car receives its own individual number in sequence. Though the format of the body/chassis number has been changed for the Corvette several times it will, at the very least, indicate the year of production and when the car was assembled relative to others during the same model year.

The **body/chassis number** is stamped into a plate which is attached to the body of each Corvette. The location of the plate varies with different years.

From 1953 through early 1960, the plate was attached to the driver's side door post. Most 1960 and all 1961 through 1962 models have the plate attached to the steering column in the engine compartment. The 1963 through 1967 models have the plate attached to the instrument support brace under the glove box. The serial plate for 1968 and newer Corvettes is attached to the dash panel or windshield post. visible through the windshield.

In addition to the serial plate, the body/chassis number is also stamped into the frame in several locations in most Corvettes. From early 1960 on. the sequential portion of the number is also stamped into the engine block. on a pad just forward of the passenger-side engine head.

Except for 1955. the **body/chassis number** does not reveal which engine a Corvette has. until 1972 when the number format was revised to include a letter which was coded to engine type.

## Engine Numbers

When a Corvette V-8 engine block is cast at a foundry, two important numbers become an integral part of the casting. One is a seven digit GM part number which appears as a uniform. raised numerical series located on the top rear, driver's side of the engine block. In the tables, this number is referred to as the **engine casting number**. The number remains the same for similar series of blocks. For some Corvette years, the same engine casting number will appear on all engines, regardless of horsepower. In some cases, the same blocks are interchangeable with Chevrolet passenger cars. Therefore, verification of this number does not necessarily indicate the correctness or originality of a Corvette engine installation.

Another important number is cast into the block at the foundry. This number is smaller than the **engine casting number** and more rough in appearance. This is because it is changed daily to correspond to the date of casting. The code usually appears as three or four characters, a letter followed by numbers. The letter indicates the month of casting. The day is indicated by the first one or two numbers. The last number indicates the year. Thus, A122 would appear on a block cast on January 12, 1962 (or 1972). The code for "small" blocks is on the top rear, passenger-side of the block. For "big" blocks, it is forward of the starter by the freeze plug on the passenger side.

When a Corvette engine is assembled at a Chevrolet engine plant, an important number is stamped into the engine block, on a pad just forward of the passenger-side engine head. This number is usually seven or more characters. The first character is alphabetic and signifies the manufacturing plant location. The next four digits are numerical and indicate month and date of engine assembly. The last one or more characters are alphabetic and designate the intended use of the engine. The last alphabetic characters are referred to as **"engine suffix"** in our tables for Corvette V-8 engines, and are almost always unique to Corvette usage. A stamped engine number of F0112RF would translate to a Corvette fuel injected engine (RF), built on the 12th day (12), of January (01), at the Flint (F) engine plant. Other engine codes are V for another Flint plant and T for Tonawanda.

Considerable emphasis is placed by Corvette enthusiasts on engine/chassis originality and, because of this, "counterfeit" cars with number alterations are becoming more common. Absolute authenticity is nearly impossible to determine, but knowledge of the chassis and engine numbering systems can reduce risk to a minimum. Remember that:

(1) 1959 and older Corvettes have many identification numbers, but the chassis was not directly keyed to the engine when the car was assembled.

(2) 1960 and newer Corvettes have digits of the body/chassis serial number stamped into the engine block during final vehicle assembly.

(3) When a Corvette engine is assembled, it is stamped with a source, date, and usage code. The stamping "pad" location is the same as later used for stamping the sequential portion of the body/chassis number during vehicle assembly.

(4) When the block for a Corvette engine is cast, it receives a part number and a date code. Verification of the part number will not determine specific correctness, but will indicate that the engine is from the correct "family". The date code should pre-date the final engine assembly date.

Several other numbers are listed in our table for other "bolt on" engine components, especially for earlier Corvettes. Many of these numbers are important, particularly in concours events, but the originality of the engine block is by far the most important consideration.

# Options

This section should be read with caution. Practically every piece of GM literature contains some type of disclaimer as " . . . accurate at press time, but manufacturer reserves right to change options and prices without notice." The purpose of the wording is obvious. Prices and options do change, and not just at model change time. There have been Corvette model years when suggested prices have changed four times. Manufacturing problems, both within GM and at supplying vendors, may cause listed options never to be available. Public demand may force an option to be listed mid-year but that option may never appear in promotional literature.

The data for the options tables was assembled from the inputs of several sources. Wherever possible, early production information was used. In some cases options advertised, but not actually installed in Corvettes, are included with explaining footnotes.

Starting in 1967, Chevrolet attached an option list to the top of Corvette gas tanks during assembly. Provided the list has not been removed, verification of original factory-installed options can be made by dropping the tank on 1967 and later models. (Viewing the list may also be possible by just detaching the rubber seal around the fuel filler) Other than original purchase information, positive verification is difficult for earlier models.

Emission controls required by the Federal Government have usually been included in the base cost of Corvettes. Regional requirements, such as for California and high altitude areas, are usually not included in base costs since these typically exceed Federal standards. For example, most 1966 Corvettes in California were equipped with Air Injector Reactors (RPO K19) which cost customers an extra $47.55 retail. California requirements for 1973 Corvettes included a $15.00 assembly line emissions test (RPO YA7), and certification (RPO VJ9), a no-charge "option." Because of the regional aspects of emissions equipment and yearly fluctuations, this information is not included in the option tables.

# Colors

Some controversy will always exist regarding factory available colors for Corvettes. This is especially true for the 1962 and older Corvette models.

Prior to the 1963 model Corvette, no paint identification coding was affixed to the Corvette body. Thus, if an earlier Corvette is re-painted carefully enough, the color can be changed without detection. Easier said than done, and most repaint can be recognized if inspected closely enough. But the lack of positive ID plate verification keeps the paint controversy brewing.

The "code" listed in the tables is the exterior color code stamped on a plate which is affixed to Corvette bodies starting in 1963. The plate is on the dash support member under the glove box in 1963 through 1967 models, and on the driver's side door post in 1968 and newer models.

Chevrolet has always used lacquer for the exterior body surfaces of Corvettes. 1957 and older Corvettes were painted with nitrocellulose lacquer, except for Inca Silver models which were acrylic lacquer. All 1958 and newer Corvette models were factory painted with acrylic lacquer. For refinishing, the acrylic colors are generally available from most major suppliers. The nitrocellulose colors can be a problem, since many paint formulas for the older colors have been pulled from local suppliers by paint manufacturers. The Corvette enthusiast has the choice of cross-referencing to an acrylic equivalent, or using original nitrocellulose lacquer supplied by vendors who service the antique auto market.

In using the "interiors" portion of the tables, it should be remembered that the interior-exterior combinations listed were not necessarily the only ones available. The combinations were generally limited in earlier years to those specified by Chevrolet, but in later years the combinations are only factory recommendations. If a customer wished a light blue '78 with a red interior he could have it, provided the dealer marked the order blank to indicate a non-recommended customer preference.

Color availability often changes. Some colors listed by Chevrolet for Corvettes were never used, while others not listed have. For instance, the Saffron exterior color listed for the 1978 Corvette was withdrawn before production and replaced with Mahogany. Another problem is that many published listings of Corvette colors are incomplete. A flagrant example is the often printed list of three 1963 exterior colors, red, blue, and silver. Actually, there were seven exterior colors available. Even GM's dealer parts books are incorrect.

## Summary and Caution

This publication, especially the section to follow, is intended to promote the fun and enjoyment of the Corvette hobby by presenting useful information in a readily accessible format. A great deal of effort has been expended in compiling the data and verifying it, including checking by many of the country's foremost Corvette enthusiasts prior to publication.

But almost nothing is absolute in the world of automobiles, especially Corvettes. A very high percentage of the following data is accurate for a high percentage of Corvettes, but exceptions are possible in almost every category.

Because of the very nature of auto production, a totally accurate listing of automotive facts, particularly related to part numbers, is impossible. General Motors does not document every production change made. The replacement parts aspect of General Motors is keyed to function, not originality. Parts are interchanged during production when shortages occur. New parts inventories are not always phased in so that all "old" parts are used before new.

The information in the tables to follow has been obtained from hundreds of sources. The sources range from published General Motors documents to surveys taken by organizations like The National Corvette Restorer's Society. Some of the data has never before been published. Information derived from surveys and observation tends to be accurate but not necessarily totally inclusive since it is based on a sampling of vehicles.

In short, you should never rely on published data as the final guideline in determining a Corvette's value. It can be helpful to you, but in the end you must balance it with good judgement, logic, and common sense.

Because of the possibility of errors, exceptions, or other reasons for inaccuracy, Michael Bruce Associates Inc. disclaims all responsibility for the accuracy of all information presented within this publication.

# 1953 CORVETTE

Production: 300

## 1953 SERIAL NUMBERS

**Body and Chassis:** E53F001001 through E53F001300
**Engine Serial:** LAY prefix
**Block Casting:** 3701481
**Head Casting:** 3836066
**Distributor:** 1112314
**Generator:** 1102793
**Starter:** 1107109 (2-coil), 1107075 (service)
**Carburetors:** Carter YH2066S (early)
　　　　　　　Carter YH2066SA (late)

● Headlight rim and bucket components are numbered in matched sets for assembly. However, the assembly numbers do not necessarily correspond exactly to the serial number of the car. (early)

## 1953 FACTS

● 1953 models have two interior hood releases, one for each latch.

● 1953 models have "short" exhaust extensions.

● Approximately the first 25 Corvettes made in 1953 had the "dome" wheel covers common to Chevrolet passenger cars. These were used while waiting for delivery of the regular Corvette covers.

● Standard Corvette production wheel covers (1953-1955) are single stamped discs with two chrome "spinner" ornaments attached parallel to a central Chevrolet Bow Tie emblem. An estimated 25 sets of caps were made with the spinner mounted perpendicular. These are rare and expensive.

● Early wheel discs have spinners which are plated brass forgings, but suppliers later changed to plated zinc die castings.

● General Motors recently stamped several hundred "new" wheel discs for 1953-1955 Corvettes. They do not have the spinners or the indentations where the spinners mount.

● Wire wheels were not available, although some 1953 Corvettes were so equipped by dealers.

● Only the 1953 model came with black oil cloth window storage bags.

● Antennas were standard on all 1953 Corvettes and consist of a mesh screen fiberglassed into the inside surface of the trunk lid.

● 1953 parking brake brackets are painted red. 1954 and later are black.

● 1953 trunk lids do not have moisture absorbant container for license recess found in 1954 and 1955 models.

● 1953 models have three separate "bullet" style air cleaners.

● Early 1953 models (up to #175) use a foot operated windshield washer assembly. Later are vacuum operated.

- The valve cover of the 1953 Corvette is a unique variation of the standard 1953 Chevrolet passenger car cover. The Corvette version is flattened at the forward end for hood clearance. The cover differs from later years by its dual central hold-down bolts. Later covers are held by bolts around the periphery. The 1953 cover has the words "Blue Flame" on the passenger side and "Special" on the driver side.

- 1953 valve covers are finished in blue-green engine enamel.

- The radiator surge tank of the 1953 and early 1954 models is unique. Its surface is smooth but later units have rigidity bands stamped in.

- Early 1953 models use a unique gas filler door. Later units were redesigned for better access. The change occurred between models #83 and #91.

- The 1953 carburetor connecting linkage is a one-piece stamping.

- The location of the fuel filter in the 1953 model is in the fuel line, just forward of the front carburetor.

- Of the 300 1953 Corvettes made, about 225 are accounted for today. Both the third and fourth Corvettes off the Flint assembly line are alive and well in the hands of private owners. The first and second Corvettes made are missing. Rumors and stories never cease, but the most commonly accepted explanation of the whereabouts of the first two Corvettes is that they were both sent to Chevrolet Engineering for testing and eventual destruction. However, conclusive documents supporting their destruction have never been located.

- 1953 exhaust valves are shorter than later models.

- 1953 brake and fuel lines run outside the chassis frame. Later models, starting early in 1954 production, run along the inside.

- Ignition shielding in the 1953 model consists of upper and lower formed metal shields. They are painted, not plated.

- The starters in the 1953 model use a two-field coil.

- The road draft tube in most 1953's has a smooth top surface. Some 1953's and all later units have an "X" stamped in for flex resistance.

- 1953 trunk mats are unique to the year, being slightly smaller than later years. The mat number is #4636966.

## 1953 OPTIONS

| RPO # | DESCRIPTION | RETAIL $ |
|-------|-------------|----------|
| 2934 | Base Corvette Convertible | 3498.00 |
| 101A | Heater | 91.40 |
| 101B | Signal Seeking AM Radio | 145.15 |

- Prices shown include federal excise taxes. Local taxes and dealer charges were not included and varied throughout the country.

- Although listed as options, both the heater and radio were installed in all 1953 Corvettes built.

- All 1953 Corvettes were equipped with whitewall tires.

- Tinted windows were not available.

## 1953 COLORS

| CODE | EXTERIOR | SOFT TOP | WHEELS | INTERIOR |
|------|----------|----------|--------|----------|
| None | Polo White | Black | Red | Red |

# 1954 CORVETTE

Production: 3,640

## 1954 SERIAL NUMBERS

**Body and Chassis:** E54S001001 through E54S004640

**Engine Serial:** F54YG suffix

**Block Casting:** 3835911

**Head Casting:** 3836241

**Distributor:** 1112314

**Generator:** 1102793

**Starter:** 1107109 early (2-coil), 1108035 later (4-coil)

**Carburetors:** Carter YH2066SA

## 1954 FACTS

• Early production 1954 models have two interior hood releases. Later models have a single interior release which activates both hood latches.

• The window storage bag for the 1954 is color keyed to the car's interior (red or beige). The design is more square in shape than the previous model. The 1954 type also has a strap which permits it to be anchored to the forward vertical trunk panel.

• The 1954 Corvette valve cover is similar to the redesigned 1954 Chevrolet passenger car cover. Both are attached to the head by stovebolts around the cover's periphery. In the case of the Corvette, the valve covers can be either chrome plated or finished in engine enamel blue. The painted Corvette cover has the decals "Blue Flame" and "150" reading from the passenger side.

• The radiator surge tank of the 1954 Corvette, except for very early models, has two rigidity bands formed in the tank. All tanks are chrome plated.

• 1954 Corvettes have vacuum operated windshield washer systems which are activated by pushing a button on the windshield wiper switch.

• The 1954 carburetor connecting linkage is a fabricated three-piece link.

• The 1954 fuel filter is mounted on the right side of the engine block adjacent to the fuel pump.

• 1954 brake and fuel lines are routed inside the frame members, except for very early models.

• Ignition shielding in the 1954 model consists of upper and lower formed metal shields. They can be painted or chrome plated. Although most 1954 models are now seen with both the valve cover and shielding chrome plated, or both units painted, the factory did not necessarily assemble the shields and covers as matched finish sets. Combinations of plated and painted units exist.

• The starters in the 1954 models use four-field coils, except for very early production models.

• The road draft tube in the 1954 model has an "X" stamped in the top surface for rigidity. Most used in 1953 were smooth.

• Early 1954 models (up to #2523) have "short" exhaust extensions. Later models have a longer type with built-in baffles. All are stainless steel.

• Early 1954 models have the "bullet" air cleaners common to the 1953 model. Models later than #2906 have the dual "pot" apparatus, designed in part to reduce the chance of engine fires.

• The "Blue Flame Six" engine used in all 1954 Corvettes carries a rating of either 150 or 155 HP. The higher horsepower was a running change made during 1954 by revising the camshaft design. Externally the engines are the same, but the more powerful version can be detected by inspecting the camshafts. The later camshafts have three dots between #5 and #6 inlet cam lobes.

• All 1954 Corvettes have six volt electrical systems.

• 1954 radios are the same as 1953 except that during 1954 the tuning face received 640 and 1240 KC Conelrad national defense markings.

• All 1954 soft tops are tan canvas with top bows painted to match.

## 1954 OPTIONS

| RPO # | DESCRIPTION | RETAIL $ |
|-------|-------------|----------|
| 2934 | Base Corvette Convertible | 2774.00 |
| 100Q | Directional Signal, Polo White | 16.75 |
| 100R | Directional Signal, Pennant Blue | 16.75 |
| 101A | Heater | 91.40 |
| 102A | Signal Seeking AM Radio | 145.15 |
| 290B | Whitewall Tires, 6.70x15 | 26.90 |
| 313M | Powerglide Automatic Transmission | 178.35 |
| 420A | Parking Brake Alarm | 5.65 |
| 421A | Courtesy Light | 4.05 |
| 422A | Windshield Washer | 11.85 |

• Prices shown include federal excise taxes. Local taxes and dealer charges are not included and varied. Prices effective October 28, 1954.

• The options list would seem to imply that a manual transmission was included in the base cost of the 1954 Corvette since the automatic is listed as an option, which was not the case. All 1954 models had the automatic.

## 1954 COLORS

| CODE | EXTERIOR | SOFT TOP | WHEELS | INTERIOR |
|------|----------|----------|--------|----------|
| None | Polo White | Beige | Red | Red |
| None | Pennant Blue | Beige | Red | Beige |
| None | Sportsman Red | Beige | Red | Red |
| None | Black | Beige | Red | Red |

• The four colors shown are those known to have been used for 1954 Corvettes. White and blue were the main colors used (especially white) and together account for about 95% of the 1954 Corvettes built. Estimates of red usage are about 3%. Many enthusiasts believe that a handful of 1954 models were painted other colors. Part of this belief results from the existence of paint availability bulletins which indicate that several other colors were available. Also, some individuals claim to have genuine examples of factory original 1954 Corvettes with colors other than white, blue, red or black. The additional colors thought to have been available include Metallic Green and Metallic Bronze.

# 1955 CORVETTE

Production: 700

## 1955 SERIAL NUMBERS

Body and Chassis: VE55S001001 through VE55S001700*
Engine Serial: F55YG suffix (6 cylinder)
F55FG suffix (V-8 with powerglide)
F255GR suffix (V-8 with manual transmission)
Block Casting: 3835911 (6 cylinder)
3703524 (V-8)
Head Casting: 3836241 (6 cylinder)
Distributor: 1112314 (6 cylinder)
1110855, 1110847 (V-8)
Generator: 1102793 (6 cylinder)
1102025 (V-8)
Starter: 1108035 (6 cylinder-4 coil)
1107627, 1107645 (V-8)
Carburetors: Carter YH2066SA (6 cylinder)
Carter WCFB 2218S, 2351S, 2366S, 3769S (V-8)

*The majority of 1955 models were equipped with V-8 engines and the body and chassis number carries a "V" prefix as indicated above. 1955 models equipped with the six cylinder engines do not have this prefix. 1955 is thus the only vintage Corvette year with a body/chassis number that identifies the type of engine installed. 1955 is also the only model year ever available with both six and eight cylinder engines.

## 1955 FACTS

• Total production of the 1955 model Corvette was 700 units. According to published data by the NCRS, of the last 555 models built (79% of total production) only six were equipped with the six cylinder engine.

• Externally, the six and eight cylinder models are similar, but the eight can be identified by a modification to the "Chevrolet" side identification consisting of an enlarged gold "V".

• Six cylinder 1955 model Corvettes are virtual duplicates of the 1954 models and still have the six-volt electrical system. The V-8 models have 12-volt systems.

• The V-8 engine offered in the 1955 Corvette was a 265CI modification of the Chevrolet passenger car engine introduced the same year. It is equipped with four-barrel carburetor, automatic choke and longer mufflers than previous six cylinder models. Horsepower was listed as 195.

• V-8 ignition shielding consists of chrome distributor and coil covers with bails, braided and grounded plug wires, and wire carriers behind the exhaust manifolds.

• V-8 engines equipped with the heater option had a manual heater cutoff valve located along the inner fender, spliced into the upper heater hose.

14

- Valve covers on the 1955 V-8 models are chrome plated with the Chevrolet script. They are held in place by four Phillips-head screws. The six cylinder valve covers are the same as 1954.
- Windshield washer activation in 1955 V-8 models is by floor pedal with coordinator.
- Hardtops were not available from the factory for the 1955 model (or the 1953-54), but several aftermarket tops were marketed, some through Chevrolet dealers.

## 1955 OPTIONS

| RPO # | DESCRIPTION | RETAIL $ |
|---|---|---|
| 2934-6 | Base Corvette Convertible—6 Cylinder | 2774.00 |
| 2934-8 | Base Corvette Convertible—8 Cylinder | 2909.00 |
| 100Q | Directional Signal, Polo White | 16.75 |
| 100R | Directional Signal, Pennant Blue | 16.75 |
| 101A | Heater | 91.40 |
| 102A | Signal Seeking AM Radio | 145.15 |
| 290B | Whitewall Tires, 6.70x15 | 26.90 |
| 313M/N | Powerglide Automatic Transmission | 178.35 |
| 420A | Parking Brake Alarm | 5.65 |
| 421A | Courtesy Light | 4.05 |
| 422A | Windshield Washer | 11.85 |

- The base price of both the six and eight cylinder models included a manual three-speed transmission. The manual transmission was not available in early production, but some later V-8 equipped models have the standard transmission. The combination of six-cylinder and manual transmission has never been verified and it is believed that no such Corvettes were ever built.
- The V-8 engine offered in 1955 was technically not an option. Corvettes so equipped were actually separate models.
- All the options listed were mandatory purchase items with either the six or eight cylinder models except for #101A (heater), #102A (radio), and 290B (whitewall tires).

## 1955 COLORS

| CODE | EXTERIOR | SOFT TOP | WHEELS | INTERIOR |
|---|---|---|---|---|
| None | Polo White | White/Beige | Red | Red |
| None | Harvest Gold | Dark Green | Yellow | Yellow |
| None | Gypsy Red | Beige | Red | Lt Beige |
| None | Corvette Copper | White | Bronze | Dk Beige |
| None | Pennant Blue | Beige | Red | Dk Beige |

- The most confusing and controversial of all Corvette model years with regard to colors is 1955. Even though production was cut back to a mere 700 units, just how many colors were factory applied remains a mystery. The colors shown above are those indicated as being used for 1955 in GM material published in 1961.
- Also not clear are soft top colors and materials. Earlier years and some '55 models have canvas tops. Sometime during 1955, vinyl tops appeared. It is generally believed that new top colors, including white, were introduced at that time.

# 1956 CORVETTE

Production: 3,467

## 1956 SERIAL NUMBERS

Body and Chassis: E56S001001 through E56S004467

Engine Suffix: FK: 210 HP, Automatic  GR: 225 HP, Manual
GV: 210 HP, Manual  GU: 240 HP, Manual
FG: 225 HP, Automatic

Block Casting: 3720991

Head Casting: ▰ 210 HP and early 225 HP (2-bolt exhaust manifolds)
▰ 240 HP and late 225 HP (3-bolt exhaust manifolds)

Distributor: 1110872, 1110879 (225, 240 HP) 1110866, 1110869, 1110878 (210 HP)

Generator: 1102043

Carburetors: Carter WCFB 2366S, 2366SA (210 HP)
Carter WCFB 2419S (front), 2362S (rear) (225 or 240 HP)

## 1956 FACTS

• The 1956 Corvette was the first major Corvette body redesign. With the exception of the dash which remained basically intact, the 1956 was visually new. It was given roll-up windows with optional power assists, external door handles and locks, exposed headlights with chrome surround bezels (except very early models which were painted), and a new sculptured side cove treatment.

• 1956 was the first year for a factory optional hardtop. The anodized header trim made it unique to the year. On some 1956's, the anodized trim is painted top color.

• The passenger seat in the 1956 model can be adjusted, the first Corvette with this feature.

• Seat belts were available for the first time in 1956. These were not factory options, but could be purchased through dealers as a kit. The belts were grey nylon with chrome-plated quick release buckles.

• The fresh air heater which heated outside "fresh" air (as opposed to drawing air from the car's interior and reheating it) was first used in the 1956 model. But very early production 1956 models still have the recirculating 1953-1955 type.

• The AM radio in the 1956 is transistorized, also a Corvette first. The station selector bar in 1956 models is plain. Models not equipped with a radio should have a special plate covering the dash mount location.

• All authentic 1956 engine valve covers have staggered hold-down holes and attach with Phillips head screws. The 210 HP engine has painted steel covers with the Chevrolet script. The 225 and 240 HP engines have 9-rib cast alloy covers.

• 1956 came factory equipped with a higher output battery (53 AMP hour) than the previous 12-volt system.

- 1956 models with standard transmissions were factory fitted with a new clutch which used heat-treated coils to replace the diaphragm-type springs previously used.
- The windshield washer reservoir for 1956 is a blue vinyl bag.
- The 1956 Corvette was the first to come factory equipped with dual four-barrel carburetors. The proper air cleaners are buffed aluminum and have a reusable oil-wetted filter element. With the dual-fours came a cast aluminum intake manifold.
- 1956 is the first year for the dual point distributors, standard with all but the base engines.

## 1956 OPTIONS

| RPO # | DESCRIPTION | RETAIL $ |
|---|---|---|
| 2934 | Base Corvette Convertible | 2900.00 |
| 101 | Heater | 115.00 |
| 102 | Signal Seeking AM Radio | 185.00 |
| 107 | Parking Brake Signal | 5.00 |
| 108 | Courtesy Lights | 8.00 |
| 109 | Windshield Washer | 11.00 |
| 290 | Whitewall Tires, 6.70x15 | 30.00 |
| 313 | Powerglide Automatic Transmission | 175.00 |
| 419 | Auxiliary Hardtop | 200.00 |
| 426 | Electric Power Windows | 60.00 |
| 449 | Special High-Lift Camshaft | 175.00 |
| 469 | Dual Four Barrel Carburetor Equipment | 160.00 |
| 473 | Hydraulic Folding Top Mechanism | 100.00 |

- A 440 series of optional paint combinations permitted the cove area to be painted beige or silver with specified exterior colors. The cost was $18.00.
- The base price included a 265 CI, 210 HP V-8 engine with 4-barrel carburetion, a manually-operated soft top and a close ratio 3-speed manual transmission. The standard rear axle ratio with the manual transmission was 3.70:1, with a 3.27:1 optional. The optional automatic came with a 3.55:1 rear axle.
- Although not listed, heavy duty brakes may also have been available during 1956.

## 1956 COLORS

| CODE | EXTERIOR | SOFT TOP | WHEELS | INTERIOR |
|---|---|---|---|---|
| None | Onyx Black | Blk-W | Black | R |
| None | Aztec Copper | Bge-W | Copper | Bge |
| None | Cascade Green | W-Bge | Green | Bge |
| None | Arctic Blue | W-Bge | Blue | R-Bge |
| None | Venetian Red | W-Bge | Red | R |
| None | Polo White | Blk-W | R-Sil | R |

ABBREVIATIONS: Blk = Black, R = Red, Bge = Beige, W = White,

- At additional cost, fender cove areas could be factory painted in offsetting colors. Factory brochures list Silver coves for Onyx Black, Arctic Blue and Polo White exteriors. Beige coves are specified for all other exteriors.

# 1957 CORVETTE

Production: 6,339

## 1957 SERIAL NUMBERS

**Body and Chassis:** E57S100001 through E57S106339

**Engine Suffix:**

| | |
|---|---|
| EF: 220 HP, Manual | FK: 250 HP, Automatic |
| FH: 220 HP, Automatic | EG: 270 HP, Manual |
| EH: 245 HP, Manual | EL: 283 HP, Manual |
| FG: 245 HP, Automatic | EN: 283 HP, Manual |
| EM: 250 HP, Manual | (w/air intake) |

**Block Casting:** 3731548

**Head Casting:** ◤▬ All 283 HP
　　　　　　　　◢▬ All except 283 HP

**Distributor:** 1110891 (220, 245, 270 HP)
　　　　　　　1110906 (250 HP, Automatic)
　　　　　　　1110889, 1110905 (250, 283 HP Manual)
　　　　　　　1110908 (283 Manual, Special HP with tach-drive)

**Generator:** 1102043 (standard tachometer drive)
　　　　　　　1102059 (non-tach drive, special EN suffix engine)

**Carburetors:** Carter WCFB 2366SA, 2655S (220 HP)
　　　　　　　　Carter WCFB 2626S (front), 2627S (rear) (245 HP)
　　　　　　　　Carter WCFB 2613S (front), 2614S (rear) (270 HP)

**Fuel Injection:** 7014360 (early), 7014520, 7014800, 7014960

## 1957 FACTS

• The 1957 model is the first to be factory equipped with fuel injection. In its hottest form, the 1957 Corvette fuel injected engine puts out 283 HP, one horsepower for each cubic inch of displacement. Records show that 1040 fuel injected 1957 Corvettes were built.

• The optional hardtop for the 1957 Corvette has stainless steel header trim.

• The optional AM radio in the 1957 Corvette is the same as the 1956 transistorized unit, except the selector has the word "Wonderbar".

• Authentic 1957 engine valve covers have staggered hold-down holes and attach with Phillips head screws. The 220 HP engine has painted steel covers with the Chevrolet script. Optional engines use the 7 or 9-rib cast alloy covers.

• The high performance EN fuel injected engine has a tachometer mounted on the steering column and a cold air induction system. Chevrolet cautioned buyers in sales literature that this engine was not for "pleasure driving" and certain options, such as the heater, were not available when RPO 579E was ordered. The number of 579E 1957 Corvettes was 43.

• The 1957 body is a carry-over from 1956.

• The front turn lamps on 1957 models have rounded bezels on most cars but squared bezels appear on some very late in production.

# 1957 OPTIONS

| RPO # | DESCRIPTION | RETAIL $ |
|-------|-------------|----------|
| 2934 | Base Corvette Convertible | 3176.32 |
| 101 | Heater | 110.00 |
| 102 | Signal Seeking AM Radio | 185.00 |
| 107 | Parking Brake Alarm | 5.00 |
| 108 | Courtesy Lights | 8.00 |
| 109 | Windshield Washer | 11.00 |
| 276 | 5-15x5.5" Wheels | 14.00 |
| 290 | Whitewall Tires, 6.70x15 | 30.00 |
| 313 | Powerglide Automatic Transmission | 175.00 |
| 419 | Auxiliary Hardtop | 200.00 |
| 426 | Power Windows | 55.00 |
| 440 | Additional Cove Color | 18.00 |
| 469A | Optional 245 HP, 283 CI Engine (2x4 Carb) | 140.00 |
| 469B | Optional 270 HP, 283 CI Engine (2x4 Carb) | 170.00 |
| 579A | Optional 250 HP, 283 CI Engine (Fuel Inj) | 450.00 |
| 579B | Optional 283 HP, 283 CI Engine (Fuel Inj) | 450.00 |
| 579E | Optional 283 HP, 283 CI Engine (Fuel Inj) | 675.00 |
| 473 | Power Operated Folding Top Mechanism | 130.00 |
| 677 | Positraction Axle, 3.70:1 Ratio | 45.00 |
| 678 | Positraction Axle, 4.11:1 Ratio | 45.00 |
| 679 | Positraction Axle, 4.56:1 Ratio | 45.00 |
| 684 | Heavy Duty Racing Suspension | 725.00 |
| 685 | 4-Speed Transmission | 175.00 |

• Fuel Injection is thought of as a mid-year option, being available somewhere after #E57S102000, but Rochester actually began slow manufacture of FI units in October, 1956, so it is possible that a few (very few) early '57 Corvettes were factory fuel injected.

• The four-speed transmission became available on May 1, 1957. This equates to about #E57S103750.

• Automatic transmissions were not available with #469B, 579B or 579E.

• RPO 276 includes small hubcaps in place of the standard full discs. The wider rims didn't have the "bumps" to retain the full wheel cover discs.

# 1957 COLORS

| CODE | EXTERIOR | SOFT TOP | WHEELS | INTERIOR |
|------|----------|----------|--------|----------|
| None | Onyx Black | Blk-W-Bge | Black | R-Bge |
| None | Aztec Copper | Bge-W | Copper | Bge |
| None | Cascade Green | Blk-W-Bge | Green | Bge |
| None | Arctic Blue | Blk-W-Bge | Blue | R-Bge |
| None | Venetian Red | Blk-W-Bge | Red | R-Bge |
| None | Polo White | Blk-W-Bge | R-Sil | R-Bge |
| None | Inca Silver | Blk-W | Silver | R-Bge |

ABBREVIATION: Blk = Black, R = Red, Bge = Beige, W = White, Sil = Silver
• At additional cost, fender cove areas could be factory painted in offsetting colors. Factory brochures list Silver coves for Onyx Black, Arctic Blue and Polo White exteriors. Beige coves are specified for all other exteriors except Inca Silver which showed an optional white cove. But evidence suggests that all Inca Silver 1957 models were solid silver.

# 1958 CORVETTE

Production: 9,168

## 1958 SERIAL NUMBERS

Body and Chassis: J58S100001 through J58S109168

Engine Suffix:  CQ: 230 HP, Manual     CR: 250 HP, Manual
                CT: 245 HP, Manual      DH: 250 HP, Automatic
                CU: 270 HP, Manual      DJ: 245 HP, Automatic
                CS: 290 HP, Manual      DG: 230 HP, Automatic

Block Casting: 3737739, 3756519

Head Casting: ◢◣ All except 290 HP
              ◣◢ 290 HP

Distributor: 1110890 (230 HP)
             1110891 (245, 270 HP)
             1110915 (250, 275 HP)
             1110914 (290 HP, tach drive)

Generator: 1102043 (standard tachometer drive)
           1102059 (non-tach drive, 290 HP)

Carburetors: Carter WCFB 2668S, 2669S, 3059S (230 HP)
             Carter WCFB 2626S, 3181S (front-245 HP)
             Carter WCFB 2627S, 2362S (rear-245 HP)
             Carter WCFB 2613S, 3182S (front-270 HP)
             Carter WCFB 2614S (rear-270 HP)

Fuel Injection: 7014900, 7014800,
                7014960, 7014900R

## 1958 FACTS

• The 283 CI engine carried over to 1958, but horsepower in the strongest 1958 fuel injected engine was lifted to 290 HP. Just over 1000 of the 290 HP versions were built during the production year. About 500 of the mild-cam 250 HP fuel engines were made. The most popular engine was the base 230 HP which accounted for nearly 50% of 1958 production.

• All carbureted engines in 1958 were equipped with glass fuel filter bowls.

• Extensive restyling in 1958 included a new dash, new upholstery, new external fiberglass panels. The distinguishing features include dual head-lights, a louvered hood and twin chrome trunk strips.

• The 1958 interior has a large 160 mph speedometer flanked by secondary instruments. The tachometer moved directly in front of the driver. A passenger grab bar is built into the right side of the dash. A central console and seat belts were standard equipment. The door panels are two piece.

• Correct carpeting for 1958 models is low-loop rayon pile.

• Authentic 1958 valve covers have staggered hold-down holes and attach with Phillips head screws. The 230 HP engine has painted steel covers with decal. Optional engines have covers which are 7-rib cast alloy with decals.

- 1958 bumpers are anchored directly to the frame through support braces in such a way as to provide substantially more protection than earlier years.
- 1958 is the first Corvette with a 9-tooth grill. Previous years have 13 teeth.
- 1958 was the year of the switch to acrylic lacquer finishes for the Corvette. Previous years were nitrocellulose lacquer, except for Inca Silver which was also acrylic.

# 1958 OPTIONS

| RPO # | DESCRIPTION | RETAIL $ |
|-------|-------------|----------|
| 867 | Base Corvette Convertible | 3591.00 |
| 101 | Heater | 96.85 |
| 102 | Signal Seeking AM Radio | 144.45 |
| 107 | Parking Brake Alarm | 5.40 |
| 108 | Courtesy Lights | 6.50 |
| 109 | Windshield Washer | 16.15 |
| 276 | 5 15x5.5" Wheels | NC |
| 290 | Whitewall Tires, 6.70x15 | 31.55 |
| 313 | Powerglide Automatic Transmission | 188.30 |
| 419 | Auxiliary Hardtop | 215.20 |
| 426 | Electric Power Windows | 59.20 |
| 440 | Additional Cove Color | 16.15 |
| 469 | Optional 245 HP, 283 CI Engine (2x4 Carb) | 150.65 |
| 469C | Optional 270 HP, 283 CI Engine (2x4 Carb) | 182.95 |
| 579 | Optional 250 HP, 283 CI Engine (Fuel Inj) | 484.20 |
| 579D | Optional 290 HP, 283 CI Engine (Fuel Inj) | 484.20 |
| 473 | Power Operated Folding Top Mechanism | 139.90 |
| 677 | Positraction Axle, 3.70:1 Ratio | 48.45 |
| 678 | Positraction Axle, 4.11:1 Ratio | 48.45 |
| 679 | Positraction Axle, 4.56:1 Ratio | 48.45 |
| 684 | Heavy Duty Brakes and Suspension | 780.10 |
| 685 | 4-Speed Transmission | 215.20 |

- Automatic transmissions were not available with #469C or 579D.
- RPO 276 included small hubcaps in place of the standard full discs. The wheels were painted body color.

# 1958 COLORS

| CODE | EXTERIOR | SOFT TOP | WHEELS | INTERIOR |
|------|----------|----------|--------|----------|
| None | Charcoal | Blk-W | Silver | C-BG-R |
| None | Snowcrest White | Blk-W-BG | Silver | C-BG-R |
| None | Silver Blue | W-BG | Silver | C-BG |
| None | Regal Turquoise | Blk-W | Silver | C |
| None | Panama Yellow | Blk-W | Silver | C |
| None | Signet Red | Blk-W | Silver | C-R |

ABBREVIATIONS: Blk = Black, R = Red, W = White, C = Charcoal, BG = Blue-Green

- At additional cost, fender cove areas could be factory painted in offsetting colors. Factory brochures list Inca Silver coves for Charcoal, Snowcrest White and Silver Blue exteriors. Snowcrest White specified for all other colors.
- Top storage well and trunk were painted interior trim color.

# 1959 CORVETTE

Production: 9,670

## 1959 SERIAL NUMBERS

Body and Chassis: J59S100001 through J59S109670

Engine Suffix:  CQ: 230 HP, Manual     CR: 250 HP, Manual
                CT: 245 HP, Manual     DH: 250 HP, Automatic
                CU: 270 HP, Manual     DJ: 245 HP, Automatic
                CS: 290 HP, Manual     DG: 230 HP, Automatic

Block Casting: 3737739, 3756519

Head Casting: ◢◣ All

Distributor: 1110946 (230 HP)
             1110891 (245, 270 HP)
             1110915 (250 HP)
             1110914 (290 HP, tach drive)

Generator: 1101043 (standard tachometer drive)
           1102059, 1102173 (290 HP, non-tach drive)

Carburetors: Carter WCFB 2669S, 3059S, 2818S (230 HP)
             Carter WCFB 2626S, 3181S (front-245 HP)
             Carter WCFB 2627S, 2362S (rear-245 HP)
             Carter WCFB 2613S, 3182S (front-270 HP)
             Carter WCFB 2614S (rear-270 HP)

Fuel Injection: 7017200, 7017250, 7017300, 7017320

## 1959 FACTS

● Exterior 1959 styling is similar to 1958, but the 1959 does not have the hood ridges or the twin chrome trunk strips.

● Gauge lenses are concave (first year) in 1959 for easier reading. Also, the tach face was redesigned for easier reading.

● 1959 door panels were redesigned from the previous year by relocating the armrests for additional elbow room and by moving the door releases forward. Also, the 1959 door panel is one piece.

● 1959 is the first year for the "T" shifter handle with the reverse lockout to prevent accidental shifting into reverse.

● 1959 is the first year for the addition of the storage bin under the passenger grab bar. The grab bar itself is more heavily padded than the previous year.

● The seat upholstery material for 1959 models is smoother than the previous year and, for the first time in the Corvette's history, a black interior was available.

● 1959 is the last year for the cast iron clutch housing.

● 1959 seat pleats run side to side.

● The windshield washer reservoir (optional) on the 1959 model mounts on the left side for carbureted and on the right side for fuel injected engines. Right side mountings are protected by heat shields.

• In late 1959, valve covers changed from staggered holes to straight across holes. The base engine has painted steel covers with decals. The optional engines have 7-rib cast alloy covers with decals. All attach with Phillips head screws.

## 1959 OPTIONS

| RPO # | DESCRIPTION | RETAIL $ |
|---|---|---|
| 867 | Base Corvette Convertible | 3875.00 |
| — | Additional Cove Color | 16.15 |
| 101 | Heater | 102.25 |
| 102 | Signal Seeking AM Radio | 149.80 |
| 107 | Parking Brake Alarm | 5.40 |
| 108 | Courtesy Light | 6.50 |
| 109 | Windshield Washers | 16.15 |
| 261 | Sunshades | 10.80 |
| 276 | 5 15x5.5" Wheels | nc |
| 290 | Whitewall Tires, 6.70x15 | 31.55 |
| 313 | Powerglide Automatic Transmission | 199.10 |
| 419 | Auxiliary Hardtop | 236.75 |
| 426 | Electric Power Windows | 59.20 |
| 469 | Optional 245 HP, 283 CI Engine (2x4 Carb) | 150.65 |
| 469C | Optional 270 HP, 283 CI Engine (2x4 Carb) | 182.95 |
| 579 | Optional 250 HP, 283 CI Engine (Fuel Inj) | 484.20 |
| 579D | Optional 290 HP, 283 CI Engine (Fuel Inj) | 484.20 |
| 473 | Power Operated Folding Top Mechanism | 139.90 |
| 675 | Positraction Axle, Optional Ratio | 48.45 |
| 684 | Heavy Duty Brakes and Suspension | 425.00 |
| 685 | 4-Speed Transmission | 188.30 |
| 686 | Metallic Brakes | 26.90 |

• Automatic transmissions were not available with #469C or 579D.

• RPO 276 included small hubcaps in place of the standard full discs. The wheels were painted body color.

• Base price of car included choice of hard or soft top.

• 1959 is the first year of sunshade availability.

## 1959 COLORS

| CODE | EXTERIOR | SOFT TOP | WHEELS | INTERIOR |
|---|---|---|---|---|
| None | Tuxedo Black | Blk-W | Black | Blk-Blu-R |
| None | Classic Cream | Blk-W | Black | Blk |
| None | Frost Blue | W-Blu | Black | Blu-R |
| None | Crown Sapphire | W-Tur | Black | T |
| None | Roman Red | Blk-W | Black | Blk-R |
| None | Snowcrest White | Blk-W-T-Blu | Black | Blk-Blu-T-R |
| None | Inca Silver | Blk-W | Black | Blk-R |

ABBREVIATIONS: Blk = Black, R = Red, W = White, Blu = Blue, T = Turquoise

• Trunk interiors are painted interior trim colors.

• 1959 is the only year for turquoise soft top availability.

• At additional cost, fender cove areas could be factory painted in offsetting colors. Factory brochures list Inca Silver coves for Tuxedo Black and Snowcrest White exteriors. Snowcrest White coves are specified for all other colors.

# 1960 CORVETTE

Production: 10,261

## 1960 SERIAL NUMBERS

Body and Chassis: 00867S100001 through 00867S110261

Engine Suffix:
CQ: 230 HP, Manual
CT: 245 HP, Manual
CU: 270 HP, Manual
CS: 315 HP, Manual
CR: 275 HP, Manual
DJ: 245 HP, Automatic

DG: 230 HP, Automatic
CY: 275 HP, Manual
  (Alum. heads)
CZ: 315 HP, Manual
  (Alum. heads)

Block Casting: 3737739, 3756519

Head Casting: All except 315 HP / 315 HP

Distributor:
1110946 (230 HP)
1110891 (245, 270 HP)
1110915 (275 HP)
1110914 (315 HP, tach drive)

Generator:
1102043 (standard tachometer drive)
1102173 (315 HP, non-tach drive)

Carburetors:
Carter WCFB 2669S, 3059S, 2818S (230 HP)
Carter WCFB 2626S, 3181S, 2419 (front-245 HP)
Carter WCFB 2627S, 2362S (rear-245 HP)
Carter WCFB 2613S, 3182S (front-270 HP)
Carter WCFB 2614S (rear-270 HP)

Fuel Injection: 7017310, 7017200, 7017320, 7017250

## 1960 FACTS

• The 1960 was also the first year for the availability of cast aluminum heads. These were cast to the new fuel injection head design, but production quality problems associated with the casting of high silicone aluminum led to the withdrawal of the special heads from the market early in 1960.

• 1960 was the first year of availability for the aluminum radiator. Its 1960 use was limited to the high-lift cam engines.

• Because of increased horsepower ratings, only manual transmissions could be combined with the 1960 fuel injected engines. Previously, the milder fuel engines could be purchased with automatics.

• The base 1960 engine has painted steel valve covers with decals. Optional engines have the 7-rib cast alloy covers. All covers have straight across mounting holes and all attach with Phillips head screws.

• The hardtop and folding top storage areas are painted body color.

• 1960 seats have fore and aft pleats.

• The windshield washer reservoir on the 1960 model mounts on the left side for all engines except fuel injected. Fuel injected engines have reservoirs mounted on the right side.

24

# 1960 OPTIONS

| RPO # | DESCRIPTION | UNITS | RETAIL $ |
|-------|-------------|-------|----------|
| 867 | Base Corvette Convertible | 10261 | 3872.00 |
| — | Additional Cove Color | - | 16.15 |
| 101 | Heater | - | 102.25 |
| 102 | Signal Seeking AM Radio | - | 137.75 |
| 107 | Parking Brake Alarm | - | 5.40 |
| 108 | Courtesy Light | - | 6.50 |
| 109 | Windshield Washers | - | 16.15 |
| 121 | Temperature Controlled Radiator Fan | - | 21.55 |
| 261 | Sunshades | - | 10.80 |
| 276 | 5 15x5.5" Wheels | - | nc |
| 290 | Whitewall Tires, 6.70x15, 4-ply | - | 31.55 |
| 313 | Powerglide Automatic Transmission | 1765 | 199.10 |
| 419 | Auxiliary Hardtop | 5732 | 236.75 |
| 426 | Electric Power Windows | 544 | 59.20 |
| 469 | Optional 245 HP, 283 CI Engine (2x4 Carb) | - | 150.65 |
| 469C | Optional 270 HP, 283 CI Engine (2x4 Carb) | - | 182.95 |
| 579 | Optional 275 HP, 283 CI Engine (Fuel Inj) | - | 484.20 |
| 579D | Optional 315 HP, 283 CI Engine (Fuel Inj) | - | 484.20 |
| 473 | Power Operated Folding Top Mechanism | - | 139.90 |
| 675 | Positraction Axle, Optional Ratio | - | 43.05 |
| 685 | 4-Speed Transmission | 5325 | 188.30 |
| 686 | Metallic Brakes | - | 26.90 |
| 687 | Heavy Duty Brakes and Suspension | - | 333.60 |
| 1408 | 5 6.70x15 Nylon Tires | - | 15.75 |
| 1625A | 24 Gallon Fuel Tank | - | 161.40 |

• Automatic transmissions were not available with #469C, 579 or 579D.

• RPO 276 included small hubcaps in place of the standard full discs.

# 1960 COLORS

| CODE | EXTERIOR | SOFT TOP | WHEELS | INTERIOR |
|------|----------|----------|--------|----------|
| None | Tuxedo Black | Blk-W-Blu | As Body | Blk-Blu-R-T |
| None | Tasco Turquoise | Blk-W-Blu | As Body | Blk-T |
| None | Horizon Blue | Blk-W-Blu | As Body | Blk-Blu-R |
| None | Honduras Maroon | Blk | As Body | Blk |
| None | Roman Red | Blk-W | As Body | Blk-R |
| None | Ermine White | Blk-W-Blu | As Body | Blk-Blu-T-R |
| None | Sateen Silver | Blk-W-Blu | As Body | Blk-Blu-T-R |
| None | Cascade Green | Blk-W-Blu | As Body | Blk |

ABBREVIATIONS: Blk = Black, R = Red, W = White, Blu = Blue,
T = Turquoise

• At additional cost, fender cove areas could be factory painted in offsetting colors. Factory brochures list Sateen Silver coves for Tuxedo Black and Ermine White exteriors. Ermine White coves are specified for all other colors.

• The blue soft tops are of a lighter shade than the blue interiors.

• Soft top color availability may have changed during the 1960 model year from that shown on the chart.

• The 1960 Cascade Green was metallic and differed from the color of the same name used in 1956-1957.

# 1961 CORVETTE

Production: 10,939

## 1961 SERIAL NUMBERS

Body and Chassis: 10867S100001 through 10867S110939

Engine Suffix:  CQ: 230 HP, Manual          CR: 275 HP, Manual
                CT: 245 HP, Manual          DJ: 245 HP, Automatic
                CU: 270 HP, Manual          DG: 230 HP, Automatic
                CS: 315 HP, Manual

Block Casting: 3756519

Head Casting: ◣◣ All except 275 and 315 HP
              ◢◣ 275 and 315 HP

Distributor: 1111500, 1110946 (230 HP)
             1110891 (245, 270 HP)
             1110915 (275 HP)
             1110914 (315 HP, tach drive)

Generator: 1102043 (standard tachometer drive)
           1102173, 1102268 (315 HP, non-tach drive)

Carburetors: Carter WCFB 2669S, 3059S, 2818S (230 HP)
             Carter WCFB 2626S, 3181S, 2419S (front-245 HP)
             Carter WCFB 2627S, 2362S (rear-245 HP)
             Carter WCFB 2613S, 3182S (front-270 HP)
             Carter WCFB 2614S (rear-270 HP)

Fuel Injection: 7017310, 7017200, 7017320, 7017250

## 1961 FACTS

• All 1961 engines are carry over designs from 1960.

• The aluminum radiator became standard in the 1961 model. Most had separate expansion tanks, but some had tanks built into the top of the radiator.

• Though not a complete styling revision from the previous year, the 1961 model incorporated several visual differences. It is the first Corvette built without heavy "teeth" in the grill, replacing them with mesh. The forward headlight bezels are body color. The rear end for 1961 is the first to feature four taillights.

• Sometime during 1961 production, the round side-mount radiator expansion tanks began to be used.

• Interior styling for the 1961 model is similar to previous years, but more room was created by reducing the width of the transmission tunnel by 20%.

• 1961 is the first year to feature exhausts that exit below the body. All previous years exit through the body or through the bumpers.

• 1961 is the last Corvette with optional "wide white" tires.

• The 1961 door sill was a new one-piece design, replacing the two-piece of the previous year.

• The base 1961 engine has painted steel valve covers with decals. Optional engines have the 7-rib cast alloy covers. All covers have straight across mounting holes and all attach with Phillips head screws.

• The windshield washer reservoir (standard) on the 1961 model mounts on the left side for carbureted and on the right side for fuel injected engines. Right side mountings are protected by heat shields.

• 1961 is the first Corvette not to have a round nose emblem.

# 1961 OPTIONS

| RPO # | DESCRIPTION | UNITS | RETAIL $ |
|---|---|---|---|
| 867 | Base Corvette Convertible | 10939 | 3934.00 |
| — | Additional Cove Color | - | 16.15 |
| 101 | Heater | - | 102.25 |
| 102 | Signal Seeking AM Radio | - | 137.75 |
| 276 | 5 15x5.5" Wheels | - | nc |
| 290 | Whitewall Tires, 6.70x15 | - | 31.55 |
| 313 | Powerglide Automatic Transmission | 1455 | 199.10 |
| 419 | Auxiliary Hardtop | 5677 | 236.75 |
| 426 | Electric Power Windows | 700 | 59.20 |
| 441 | Direct Flow Exhaust System | - | nc |
| 469 | Optional 245 HP, 283 CI Engine (2x4 Carb) | - | 150.65 |
| 468 | Optional 270 HP, 283 CI Engine (2x4 Carb) | - | 182.95 |
| 353 | Optional 275 HP, 283 CI Engine (Fuel Inj) | - | 484.20 |
| 354 | Optional 315 HP, 283 CI Engine (Fuel Inj) | - | 484.20 |
| 473 | Power Operated Folding Top Mechanism | - | 161.40 |
| 675 | Positraction Axle, Optional Ratio | - | 43.05 |
| 685 | 4-Speed Transmission | 7012 | 188.30 |
| 686 | Metallic Brakes | - | 37.70 |
| 687 | Heavy Duty Brakes and Suspension | - | 333.60 |
| 1408 | 5 6.70x15 Nylon Tires | - | 15.75 |
| 1625 | 24 Gallon Fuel Tank | - | 161.40 |

• Automatic transmissions were not available with #468, 353 or 354.

• RPO 276 included small hubcaps in place of the standard full discs.

• Windshield washers, courtesy lights, sun shades, temperature controlled radiator fan, and parking brake warning light all became standard equipment.

# 1961 COLORS

| CODE | EXTERIOR | SOFT TOP | WHEELS | INTERIOR |
|---|---|---|---|---|
| None | Tuxedo Black | Blk-W | As Body | Blk-R-F-Blu |
| None | Ermine White | Blk-W | As Body | Blk-R-F-Blu |
| None | Roman Red | Blk-W | As Body | Blk-R |
| None | Sateen Silver | Blk-W | As Body | Blk-R-Blu |
| None | Jewel Blue | Blk-W | As Body | Blk-Blu |
| None | Fawn Beige | Blk-W | As Body | Blk-R-F |
| None | Honduras Maroon | Blk-W | As Body | Blk-F |

ABBREVIATIONS: Blk = Black, R = Red, W = White, Blu = Blue, F = Fawn

• At additional cost, fender cove areas could be factory painted in offsetting colors. Factory brochures list Sateen Silver coves for Tuxedo Black and Ermine White exteriors. Ermine White coves are specified for all other colors.

• 1961 is the only year of availability for Jewel Blue.

• 1961 is the last year of availability for optional color coves.

# 1962 CORVETTE

Production: 14,531

## 1962 SERIAL NUMBERS

Body and Chassis: 20867S100001 through 20867S114531

Engine Suffix:  RC: 250 HP, Manual       RF: 360 HP, Manual
                RD: 300 HP, Manual       SC: 250 HP, Automatic
                RE: 340 HP, Manual       SD: 300 HP, Automatic

Block Casting: 3782870

Head Casting: ◼️ 250 HP
              ◼️ All except 250 HP

Distributor: 1110984 (250, 300 HP)
             1110985 (340 HP)
             1110990, 1111011 (360 HP)

Generator: 1102268 (340, 360 HP)
           1102174 (250, 300 HP)

Carburetor: Carter WCFB 3191S (250 HP)
            Carter AFB 3269S (300, 340 HP)

Fuel Injection: 7017355, 7017360, 7017365, 7017370

## 1962 FACTS

• 1962 was the first year for the 327 CI engine lineup. The base engine has a horsepower rating of 250. The dual four-barrel carburetor engines available in Corvettes since 1956 were no longer available in 1962. Instead, large AFB carburetors were used for fuel feed in optional engines other than fuel injected.

• 1962 styling was similar to 1961, but some significant visual changes were made. Most apparent is the change in the design of the side cove area. Previously, the cove was outlined in chrome. In the 1962, it is simply outlined by a lip which is part of the molded fiberglass fender and door shapes. Because of the absence of the chrome outline, coves were no longer available in colors contrasting the body color.

• The simulated vent treatment in the cove area was changed in 1962 to a single louver. Previous models had three spears.

• 1962 is the last Corvette with an external trunk opening.

• All 1962 engines use distributor drive tachometers. The only tach-drive distributors previously used for a Corvette V-8 was on the solid lifter fuel injected engine.

• 1962 is the first narrow whitewall Corvette, using whitewalls which measure between ⅞" and 1".

• 1962 is the first Corvette to feature an aluminum transmission case for the Powerglide automatic.

• The 1962 model is the last to feature exposed headlights.

• The 1962 model is the last Corvette with a solid rear axle.

- The 250 and 300 HP engines in 1962 use painted steel valve covers with decals. 340 and 360 HP engines use 7-fin cast alloy covers with decals.
- The windshield washer reservoir on the 1962 model mounts on the left side for all engines except fuel injected. Fuel injected engines have reservoirs mounted on the right side. Right side mountings are protected by heat shields.
- 1962 was the last model year for power top availability.
- 1962 taillights have protector cones at the inside trunk surface.
- Early 1962 Corvette rocker panel moldings have no paint between the ribs. Later 1962 models have black paint between the ribs.

## 1962 OPTIONS

| RPO # | DESCRIPTION | UNITS | RETAIL $ |
|---|---|---|---|
| 867 | Base Corvette Convertible | 14531 | 4038.00 |
| 102 | Signal Seeking AM Radio | - | 137.75 |
| 276 | 5 15x5.5" Wheels | - | nc |
| 313 | Powerglide Automatic Transmission | 1525 | 199.10 |
| 419 | Auxiliary Hardtop | 8065 | 236.75 |
| 426 | Electric Power Windows | 988 | 59.20 |
| 441 | Direct Flow Exhaust System | - | nc |
| 473 | Power Operated Folding Top Mechanism | - | 139.90 |
| 488 | 24 Gallon Fuel Tank | - | 118.40 |
| 583 | Optional 300 HP, 327 CI Engine | - | 53.80 |
| 396 | Optional 340 HP, 327 CI Engine | - | 107.60 |
| 582 | Optional 360 HP, 327 CI Engine (Fuel Inj) | - | 484.20 |
| 675 | Positraction Rear Axle | - | 43.05 |
| 685 | 4-Speed Transmission | 11320 | 188.30 |
| 686 | Metallic Brakes | - | 37.70 |
| 687 | Heavy Duty Brakes and Suspension | - | 333.60 |
| 1832 | Whitewall Tires, 6.70x15 | - | 31.55 |
| 1833 | Nylon Tires, 6.70x15 | - | 15.70 |

- Automatic transmissions were not available with RPO 396 or RPO 582.
- RPO 276 included small hubcaps in place of the standard full discs.
- Heater was standard on all but export models.

## 1962 COLORS

| CODE | EXTERIOR | SOFT TOP | WHEELS | INTERIOR |
|---|---|---|---|---|
| None | Tuxedo Black | Blk-W | Blk | Blk-R |
| None | Fawn Beige | Blk-W | Blk-Bge | R-F |
| None | Roman Red | Blk-W | Blk-R | Blk-R |
| None | Ermine White | Blk-W | Blk-W | Blk-R-F |
| None | Almond Beige | Blk-W | Blk-Bge | R-F |
| None | Sateen Silver | Blk-W | Blk-Sil | Blk-R |
| None | Honduras Maroon | Blk-W | Blk-Mar | Blk-F |

ABBREVIATIONS: Blk = Black, R = Red, W = White, F = Fawn, Sil = Silver

- 1962 was the only year of availability for Almond Beige.
- All 1962 Corvettes factory equipped with whitewall tires had wheels painted black. Those equipped with blackwall tires or RPO 276 had wheels painted body color.

# 1963 CORVETTE

Production: 10,594 coupe, 10,919 convertible

## 1963 SERIAL NUMBERS

**Body and Chassis:** 30867S100001 through 30867S121513
(For coupes, first 5 digits are: 30837)

**Engine Suffix:** RC: 250 HP, Manual   RF: 360 HP, Manual
RD: 300 HP, Manual   SC: 250 HP, Automatic
RE: 340 HP, Manual   SD: 300 HP, Automatic

**Block Casting:** 3782870

**Head Casting:** 🔲 250 HP
🔲 All except 250 HP

**Distributor:** 1111024 (250, 300, 340 HP)
1111022 (360 HP)

**Carburetor:** Carter WCFB 3501S, 3500S (250 HP)
Carter AFB 3460S, 3461S (300, 340 HP)

**Fuel Injection:** 7017375

## 1963 FACTS

● 1963 is the only year for the "split window" coupe body style. For visibility reasons, the split was removed from the rear window of the 1964.

● The instruments in the 1963 are unique to the year. They have black faces with deep aluminum finish recesses.

● The 1963 model is the first year for knock-off aluminum wheels. The wheels were finished with bright center cones and unpainted rib sections. Both two and three prong hubs were offered. Some enthusiasts believe the wheels were "over the counter" only in 1963 and not factory installed.

● The 1963 door is unique to the 1963-1967 series in that it has both a stainless steel molding forward of the vent window and raised "pads" for the exterior door handles. All but late 1964's had the pads, but not the molding.

● The 1963 model is the only one of the 1963-1967 series with an adjustable bottom seat angle mechanism built in.

● Early 1963 models have storage wells under the seats, but the feature was removed at about the middle of production.

● Most 1963 models have fiberglass headlight buckets. A few 1963 models and all of the 1964-1967 Corvettes have metal buckets.

● The glove box door in the 1963 is fiberglass. Later models are metal.

● The face plate on the glove box door of 1963 Corvettes is covered with clear plastic. Later years are not.

● Two gas filler doors were used during 1963. Early cars have a pin and guide mechanism while later models and all 1964-1967 models have a simple hinge and slide catch.

● The 1963 hood is unique, having rectangular trim panels mounted in two forward recesses.

# 1963 OPTIONS

| RPO # | DESCRIPTION | UNITS* | RETAIL $ |
|-------|-------------|--------|----------|
| 837 | Base Corvette Sport Coupe | 10594 | 4257.00 |
| 867 | Base Corvette Convertible | 10919 | 4037.00 |
| 898 | Genuine Leather Seat Trim | - | 80.70 |
| 941 | Sebring Silver Exterior Paint | - | 80.70 |
| A01 | Soft Ray Tinted Glass, All Windows | - | 16.15 |
| A02 | Soft Ray Tinted Glass, Windshield Only | - | 10.80 |
| A31 | Electric Power Windows | 3742 | 59.20 |
| C07 | Auxiliary Hardtop (for roadster) | 5732 | 236.75 |
| C48 | Heater and Defroster Deletion (credit) | - | -100.00 |
| C60 | Air Conditioning | 278 | 421.80 |
| G81 | Positraction Rear Axle, All Ratios | 17554 | 43.05 |
| G91 | Special Highway 3.08:1 Axle (not posi) | - | 2.20 |
| J50 | Power Brakes | 3336 | 43.05 |
| J65 | Sintered Metallic Brakes | - | 37.70 |
| L75 | Optional 300 HP, 327 CI Engine | - | 53.80 |
| L76 | Optional 340 HP, 327 CI Engine | - | 107.60 |
| L84 | Optional 360 HP, 327 CI Engine (Fuel Inj) | - | 430.40 |
| M20 | 4-Speed Transmission | 17973 | 188.30 |
| M35 | Powerglide Automatic Transmission | 2621 | 199.10 |
| N03 | 36 Gallon Fuel Tank (coupe only) | - | 202.30 |
| N11 | Off Road Exhaust System | - | 37.70 |
| N34 | Woodgrained Plastic Steering Wheel | - | 16.15 |
| N40 | Power Steering | 3063 | 75.35 |
| P48 | Special Cast Aluminum Knock-Off Wheels | - | 322.80 |
| P91 | Blackwall Nylon Tires, 6.70x15, 4-ply | - | 15.70 |
| P92 | Whitewall Rayon Tires, 6.70x15, 4-ply | 19383 | 31.55 |
| T86 | Back-Up Lamps | - | 10.80 |
| U65 | Signal Seeking AM Radio (early) | >20362 | 137.75 |
| U69 | AM-FM Radio (early) | | 174.35 |
| Z06 | Special Performance Equip for Coupe (early) | 199 | 1818.45 |

*Sales during production year according to Chevrolet records.

• RPO 898 leather seat trim available in saddle only.

• Powerglide transmissions not available with RPO L76 or L84

• RPO Z06 available in coupes only early in production; coupes or roadsters late in production. Late option cost of $1,293.95 excluded KO wheels and 36 gallon tank.

# 1963 COLORS

| CODE | EXTERIOR | SOFT TOP | WHEELS | INTERIORS GM SUGGESTED |
|------|----------|----------|--------|------------------------|
| 900 | Tuxedo Black | Blk-W-Bge | Blk | Blk-R-S |
| 936 | Ermine White | Blk-W-Bge | Blk | Blk-R-S-DB |
| 923 | Riverside Red | Blk-W-Bge | Blk | Blk-R-S |
| 912 | Silver Blue | Blk-W-Bge | Blk | Blk-DB |
| 916 | Daytona Blue | Blk-W-Bge | Blk | R-S-DB |
| 932 | Saddle Tan | Blk-W-Bge | Blk | Blk-R-S |
| 941 | Sebring Silver | Blk-W-Bge | Blk | Blk-R-S-DB |

• Wheels of 63's with blackwall tires may have been painted body color.

Interior Codes: Blk/V=std; R/V=490C coupe, 490D conv; DB/V=490A coupe, 490B conv; S/V=490E coupe, 490F conv; S/L=898A coupe, 898B conv. Note: Additional interior codes were used in 1963.
ABBREVIATIONS: Blk=Black, R=Red, W=White, S=Saddle, DB=Dark Blue, Bge=Beige, L=Leather, V=Vinyl

# 1964 CORVETTE

Production: 8,304 coupe, 13,925 convertible

## 1964 SERIAL NUMBERS

Body and Chassis: 40867S100001 through 40867S122229
(For coupes, first 5 digits are: 40837)

Engine Suffix:
| | |
|---|---|
| RC: 250 HP, Manual | RT: 365 HP, Manual/T-Ign |
| RD: 300 HP, Manual | RU: 365 HP, Manual/T-Ign/AC |
| RE: 365 HP, Manual | RX: 375 HP, Manual/T-Ign |
| RF: 375 HP, Manual | SC: 250 HP, Automatic |
| RP: 250 HP, Manual/AC | SD: 300 HP, Automatic |
| RQ: 300 HP, Manual/AC | SK: 250 HP, Automatic/AC |
| RR: 365 HP, Manual/AC | SL: 300 HP, Automatic/AC |

Block Casting: 3782870

Head Casting: ◣▬ 250 HP
◣▬ All except 250 HP

Distributor: 1111024 (250, 300 HP)     1111063, 1111070 (375 HP)
1111062, 1111069 (365 HP)  1111064 (375 HP, T-Ign)
1111060 (365 HP, T-Ign)

Carburetor: Carter WCFB 3501S, 3500S, (250 HP)
Carter AFB 3720S, 3721S (300 HP)
Holly R2818A (365 HP)

Fuel Injection: 7017375R, 7017380

## 1964 FACTS

• 1964 styling is very similar to 1963. Changes include replacement of the divided rear window in coupes with a single window, removal of the hood trim panels (the depressions in the hood remained, but not the recesses for the trim panels, making the 1964 hood unique to the year.

• 1964 instruments are similar to 1963 except that the center recess areas are black in the 1964 model.

• The seats in the 1964 Corvette are unique to the year. They are similar to the 1963, but have no built-in rake adjusting mechanism for the lower cushion and they are broader at the top of the back cushion.

• The 1964 optional knock-off wheels are the same as the 1963 model, with bright center cones and unpainted rib sections, but only the three prong knock-off hub was available in 1964.

• The steering wheel in the 1964 model is walnut grain plastic.

• A fan was added to the rear area of the 1964 coupes to assist with the ventilation problem common to 1963 models. The operating switch for the three-speed fan is located under the driver side dash. The external openings for the vent are located on the side of the roof, between the door and rear window. The driver's side is functional. The passenger side is not.

• The 1964 door is unique, having the raised "pad" for door handle mounting, but not the stainless steel molding forward of the vent window like the 1963. The pad is missing from very late '64 models.

# 1964 OPTIONS

| RPO # | DESCRIPTION | UNITS* | RETAIL $ |
|-------|-------------|--------|----------|
| 837 | Base Corvette Sport Coupe | 8304 | 4252.00 |
| 867 | Base Corvette Convertible | 13925 | 4037.00 |
| — | Genuine Leather Seat Trim | 1334 | 80.70 |
| A01 | Soft Ray Tinted Glass, All Windows | 6031 | 16.15 |
| A02 | Soft Ray Tinted Glass, Windshield Only | 6387 | 10.80 |
| A31 | Electric Power Windows | 3706 | 59.20 |
| C07 | Auxiliary Hardtop (for roadster) | 7023 | 236.75 |
| C48 | Heater and Defroster Deletion (credit) | 60 | −100.00 |
| C60 | Air Conditioning ( not available with L84) | 1988 | 421.80 |
| F40 | Special Front and Rear Suspension | - | 37.70 |
| G81 | Positraction Rear Axle, All Ratios | 18279 | 43.05 |
| G91 | Special Highway 3.08:1 Axle | 2310 | 2.20 |
| J50 | Power Brakes | 2270 | 43.05 |
| J56 | Special Sintered Metallic Brake Package | 29 | 629.50 |
| J65 | Sintered Metallic Brakes (power) | 4780 | 53.80 |
| K66 | Transistor Ignition System | 552 | 75.35 |
| L75 | Optional 300 HP, 327 CI Engine | 10471 | 53.80 |
| L76 | Optional 365 HP, 327 CI Engine | 7171 | 107.60 |
| L84 | Optional 375 HP, 327 CI Engine (Fuel Inj) | 1325 | 538.00 |
| M20 | 4-Speed Transmission | 19024 | 188.30 |
| M35 | Powerglide Automatic ( n/a with L76 or L84) | 2480 | 199.10 |
| N03 | 36 Gallon Fuel Tank (coupe only) | 38 | 202.30 |
| N11 | Off Road Exhaust System | 1953 | 37.70 |
| N40 | Power Steering | 3126 | 75.35 |
| P48 | Special Cast Aluminum Knock-Off Wheels | 806 | 322.80 |
| P91 | Blackwall Nylon Tires, 6.70x15 | - | 15.70 |
| P92 | Whitewall Rayon Tires, 6.70x15 | 19977 | 31.85 |
| T86 | Back Up Lamps | 11085 | 10.80 |
| U69 | AM-FM Radio | 20934 | 176.50 |

*Sales during production year according to Chevrolet records.
• RPO-J56 and RPO-F40 available only with 375 HP, 4-speed transmission

# 1964 COLORS

| CODE | EXTERIOR | SOFT TOP | WHEELS | INTERIORS GM SUGGESTED |
|------|----------|----------|--------|------------------------|
| 900 | Tuxedo Black | Blk-W-Bge | Black | Blk-R-Sil-W |
| 936 | Ermine White | Blk-W-Bge | Black | Blk-R-DB-S-Sil-W |
| 923 | Riverside Red | Blk-W-Bge | Black | Blk-R- W |
| 940 | Satin Silver | Blk-W-Bge | Black | Blk-R-DB-Sil-W |
| 912 | Silver Blue | Blk-W-Bge | Black | Blk-DB-W |
| 916 | Daytona Blue | Blk-W-Bge | Black | DB-Sil-W |
| 932 | Saddle Tan | Blk-W-Bge | Black | S-W |

Interior Codes: Blk/V=std; Blk/L=898A; R/V=490AA coupe, 490AB conv; R/L=898EA coupe, 898FA conv; DB/V=490BA coupe, 490BB conv; DB/L=898JA coupe, 898KA conv; S/V=490CA coupe, 490CB conv; S/L=898CA coupe, 898DA conv; Sil/Blk/V=491AA coupe, 491AE conv; Sil/Blk/L=899AA coupe, 899AE conv; Sil/DB/V=491BA coupe, 491BE conv; Sil/DB/L=899BA coupe, 899BE conv; W/Blk/V=491CA coupe, 491CE conv; W/Blk/L=899CA coupe, 899CE conv; W/DB/V=491GA coupe, 491GE conv; W/DB/L=899GA coupe, 899GE conv; W/R/V=491DA coupe, 491DE conv; W/R/L=899DA coupe, 899DE conv; W/S/V=491HA coupe, 491HE conv; W/S/L=899HA coupe, 899HE conv. Additional interior codes were used .

ABBREVIATIONS: Blk = Black, R = Red, W = White, S = Saddle, DB = Dark Blue, Bge = Beige, Sil = Silver, L=Leather, V=Vinyl

# 1965 CORVETTE

Production: 8,186 coupe, 15,376 convertible

## 1965 SERIAL NUMBERS

Body and Chassis: 194675S100001 through 194675S123562
(For coupes, first 6 digits are: 194375)

| Engine Suffix: | | |
|---|---|---|
| HE: 250 HP, Manual | | HO: 250 HP, Automatic |
| HF: 300 HP, Manual | | HP: 300 HP, Automatic |
| HG: 375 HP, Manual | | HQ: 250 HP, Automatic/AC |
| HH: 365 HP, Manual | | HR: 300 HP, Automatic/AC |
| HI: 250 HP, Manual/AC | | HT: 350 HP, Manual |
| HJ: 300 HP, Manual/AC | | HU: 350 HP, Manual/AC |
| HK: 365 HP, Manual/AC | | HV: 350 HP, Manual/T-Ign |
| HL: 365 HP, Manual/T-Ign | | HW: 350 HP, Manual/T-Ign/AC |
| HM: 365 HP, Manual/T-Ign/AC | | IF: 425 HP, Manual |
| HN: 375 HP, Manual/T-Ign | | |

Block Casting: 3782870 (327 CI)
3855962 (396 CI)

Head Casting: ●◢ All 327 CI

Distributor: 1111076 (250, 300 HP)     1111070 (375 HP)
1111087 (350 HP)          1111064 (375 HP, T-Ign)
1111157 (350 HP, T-Ign)   1111093 (425 HP)
1111069 (365 HP)          1111060 (365 HP, T-Ign)

Carburetor: Carter WCFB 3696S, 3697S (250 HP)
Carter AFB 3720SA, 3721SA (300 HP)
Holley R2818A (350, 365 HP)
Holley R3124A (425 HP)

Fuel Injection: 7017380

## 1965 FACTS

● 1965 styling is similar to the previous two years, but with several significant differences. The side front fender louvers were redesigned in 1965 and made functional. The 1965 standard hood has no depressions and no trim. The 1965 grill is a horizontal bar as before, but the center bars are black and only the outer trim ring is bright (unique to the year).

● 1965 instruments are flat black, flat-face aircraft type. The dash area surrounding the radio and speaker bezel areas is a painted surface, rather than vinyl covered as previous two years. (Very early 1963 cars also had painted surfaces.)

● 1965 is the first year for Corvette disc brake availability. The system is four-wheel disc, with four-piston caliper assemblies at each wheel. Although disc brakes were standard on the 1965 model and included in the base price, drum brakes could be ordered as a delete cost option in early 1965 as long as drum brake parts remained in factory inventory.

● 1965 was the last year for the availability of fuel injection.

● The 1965 optional knock-off wheels are the same as the 1963 and 1964 type, except that the area between the fins is finished in dark grey.

34

# 1965 OPTIONS

| RPO # | DESCRIPTION | UNITS* | RETAIL $ |
|-------|-------------|--------|----------|
| 19437 | Base Corvette Sports Coupe | 8186 | 4321.00 |
| 19467 | Base Corvette Convertible | 15376 | 4106.00 |
| — | Genuine Leather Seat Trim | 2128 | 80.70 |
| A01 | Soft Ray Tinted Glass, All Windows | 8752 | 16.15 |
| A02 | Soft Ray Tinted Glass, Windshield Only | 7624 | 10.80 |
| A31 | Electric-Power Windows | 3809 | 59.20 |
| C07 | Auxiliary Hardtop (for roadsters) | 7787 | 236.75 |
| C48 | Heater and Defroster Deletion (credit) | 39 | −100.00 |
| C60 | Air Conditioning | 2423 | 421.80 |
| F40 | Special Front and Rear Suspension | 975 | 37.70 |
| G81 | Positraction Rear Axle, All Ratios | 19965 | 43.05 |
| G91 | Special Highway 3.08:1 Axle | 1886 | 2.20 |
| J50 | Power Brakes | 4044 | 43.05 |
| J61 | Drum Brake Substitution (credit) | 316 | −64.50 |
| K66 | Transistor Ignition System | 3686 | 75.35 |
| L75 | Optional 300 HP, 327 CI Engine | 8358 | 53.80 |
| L76 | Optional 365 HP, 327 CI Engine | 5011 | 129.15 |
| L78 | Optional 425 HP, 396 CI Engine | 2157 | 292.70 |
| L79 | Optional 350 HP, 327 CI Engine | 4716 | 107.60 |
| L84 | Optional 375 HP, 327 CI Engine (Fuel Inj) | 771 | 538.00 |
| M20 | 4-Speed Transmission | 21107 | 188.30 |
| M35 | Powerglide Automatic Transmission | 2021 | 199.10 |
| N03 | 36 Gallon Fuel Tank (coupe only) | 41 | 202.30 |
| N11 | Off Road Exhaust System | 2468 | 37.70 |
| N14 | Side Mount Exhaust System | 759 | 134.50 |
| N32 | Teakwood Steering Wheel | 2259 | 48.45 |
| N36 | Telescopic Steering Column | 3917 | 43.05 |
| N40 | Power Steering | 3236 | 96.85 |
| P48 | Special Cast Aluminum Knock-Off Wheels | 1116 | 322.80 |
| P92 | Whitewall Tires, 7.75x15 (rayon cord) | 19300 | 31.85 |
| T01 | Goldwall Tires, 7.75x15 (nylon cord) | 989 | 50.05 |
| U69 | AM-FM Radio | 22113 | 203.40 |
| Z01 | Backup Lamps and Inside Day/Night Mirror | 15397 | 16.15 |

*Sales during production year according to Chevrolet records.

• RPO F40 available only with L84/L78, 4-speed transmission and G81

# 1965 COLORS

| CODE | EXTERIOR | SOFT TOP | WHEELS | INTERIORS GM SUGGESTED |
|------|----------|----------|--------|------------------------|
| AA | Tuxedo Black | Blk-W-Bge | Black | ⎛ Blk-R-Blu-S ⎞ |
| CC | Ermine White | Blk-W-Bge | Black | ⎝ Sil-W-G-M ⎠ |
| FF | Nassau Blue | Blk-W-Bge | Black | Blk-Blu-W |
| GG | Glen Green | Blk-W-Bge | Black | Blk-S-W-G |
| MM | Milano Maroon | Blk-W-Bge | Black | Blk-S-W-M-R |
| QQ | Silver Pearl | Blk-W-Bge | Black | Blk-R-Sil |
| UU | Rally Red | Blk-W-Bge | Black | Blk-R-W |
| XX | Goldwood Yellow | Blk-W-Bge | Black | Blk-W |

Interior Codes: Blk/V=std; Blk/L=402; R/V=407; R/L=408; Blu/V=414; Blu/L=415; S/V=420; S/L=421; Sil/V=426; Sil/L=427; G/V=430; G/L=431; M/V=435; M/L=436; W/R/V=443; W/R/L=444; W/Blk/V=437; W/Blk/L=438; W/Blu/V=450; W/Blu/L=451.

ABBREVIATIONS: Blk = Black, R = Red, W = White, S = Saddle, Blu = Blue, Bge = Beige, Sil = Silver, M = Maroon, G = Green, L=Leather, V=Vinyl

# 1966 CORVETTE

Production: 9,958 coupe, 17,762 convertible

## 1966 SERIAL NUMBERS

Body and Chassis: 194676S100001 through 194676S127720
(For coupes, first 6 digits are: 194376)

Engine Suffix:  HE: Manual (327)                   KH: SHP, AC, A.I.R. (327)
HH: A.I.R. (327)                    HP: Power Steering (327)
HR: Automatic/A.I.R. (327)   IL: HP (427)
HD: SHP/A.I.R. (327)            IM: A.I.R. (427)
HO: Automatic (327)             IP: SHP (427)
HT: SHP (327)

A.I.R. = Air Injector Reactor (California), HP = High Performance,
SHP = Special High Performance, AC = Air Conditioning

Distributor: 1111153 (300 HP)        1111141, 1111142 (390 HP)
1111093 (425 HP)      1111156, 1111157 (350 HP)

Block Casting: 3858174 (Most 327 CI)     3869942 (427 CI)
3892657 (Late 327 CI)

Head Casting: ▆▆ All 327 CI

Carburetor: Holley R3367A, R3416A (300, 350 HP)
Holley R3370A, R3433A (390 HP)
Holley R3247A (425 HP)

## 1966 FACTS

• The 1966 model Corvette has very similar styling to the 1965 model. The differences are mainly trim, including the addition of the Corvette script (vertical style) to the hood and a new plated, square mesh style cast grill.

• The seats in 1966 models are the same as 1965 except that there are additional pleats in the upper and lower sections for better weight distribution along the seams.

• The 1966 optional knock-off wheels are similar to the design of previous years, but the center cone is a dull finish rather than bright. The area between the fins is painted a dark grey.

• 1966 is the first year for the 427 CI engine. Models equipped with this engine have a special hood.

• The exhaust bezels of the 1966 model are chrome plated alloy. Previous Sting Ray models are stainless steel.

• The fake and functional roof vents of previous years were completely eliminated on the 1966 coupe models.

• The fiberboard headliners of previous years were replaced with vinyl covered foam in 1966 coupes.

• 1966 was the first year of availability for factory headrests (optional).

• Backup lights became standard equipment with the 1966 model. They were incorporated into the existing rear lenses.

• The interior door pulls of the 1966 model are bright metal.

36

# 1966 OPTIONS

| RPO # | DESCRIPTION | UNITS* | RETAIL $ |
|---|---|---|---|
| 19437 | Base Corvette Sport Coupe | 9958 | 4295.00 |
| 19467 | Base Corvette Convertible | 17762 | 4084.00 |
| — | Genuine Leather Seats | 2002 | 79.00 |
| A01 | Soft Ray Tinted Glass, All Windows | 11859 | 15.80 |
| A02 | Soft Ray Tinted Glass, Windshield Only | 9270 | 10.55 |
| A31 | Electric Power Windows | 4562 | 59.20 |
| A82 | Headrests | 1033 | 42.15 |
| A85 | Shoulder Harness | 37 | 26.35 |
| C07 | Auxiliary Hardtop (for roadster) | 8463 | 231.75 |
| C48 | Heater and Defroster Deletion (credit) | 54 | −97.85 |
| C60 | Air Conditioning | 3520 | 412.90 |
| F41 | Special Front and Rear Suspension | 2705 | 36.90 |
| G81 | Positraction Rear Axle, All Ratios | 24056 | 42.15 |
| J50 | Power Brakes | 5464 | 43.05 |
| J56 | Special Heavy Duty Brakes | 382 | 342.30 |
| K66 | Transistor Ignition System | 7146 | 73.75 |
| L36 | Optional 390 HP, 427 Engine | 5116 | 181.20 |
| L72 | Optional 425 HP, 427 CI Engine | 5258 | 312.85 |
| L79 | Optional 350 HP, 327 CI Engine | 7591 | 105.35 |
| M20 | 4-Speed Transmission | 10837 | 184.30 |
| M21 | 4-Speed Close Ratio Transmission | 13903 | 184.30 |
| M22 | 4-Speed Close Ratio Trans., Heavy Duty | 15 | 237.00 |
| M35 | Powerglide Automatic Transmission | 2401 | 194.85 |
| N03 | 36 Gallon Fuel Tank | 66 | 198.05 |
| N11 | Off Road Exhaust System | 2795 | 36.90 |
| N14 | Side Mount Exhaust System | 3617 | 131.65 |
| N32 | Teakwood Steering Wheel | 3941 | 48.45 |
| N36 | Telescopic Steering Column | 3670 | 42.15 |
| N40 | Power Steering | 5611 | 94.80 |
| P48 | Special Cast Aluminum Knock-Off Wheels | 1194 | 326.00 |
| P92 | Whitewall Tires, 7.75x15 (rayon cord) | 17969 | 31.30 |
| T01 | Goldwall Tires, 7.75x15 (nylon cord) | 5557 | 46.55 |
| U69 | AM-FM Radio | 26363 | 199.10 |
| V74 | Traffic Hazard Lamp Switch | 5764 | 11.60 |

*Sales during production year according to Chevrolet records.

# 1966 COLORS

| CODE | EXTERIOR | SOFT TOP | WHEELS | INTERIORS GM SUGGESTED |
|---|---|---|---|---|
| 900 | Tuxedo Black | Blk-W-Bge | Black | Blk-R-BB-WB |
| 972 | Ermine White | Blk-W-Bge | Black | Sil-S-G-Blu |
| 976 | Nassau Blue | Blk-W-Bge | Black | Blk-BB-WB-Blu |
| 982 | Mosport Green | Blk-W-Bge | Black | Blk-G |
| 988 | Milano Maroon | Blk-W-Bge | Black | Blk-S |
| 986 | Silver Pearl | Blk-W-Bge | Black | Blk-Sil |
| 974 | Rally Red | Blk-W-Bge | Black | Blk-R |
| 984 | Sunfire Yellow | Blk-W-Bge | Black | Blk |
| 978 | Laguna Blue | Blk-W-Bge | Black | Blk-BB-Blu |
| 980 | Trophy Blue | Blk-W-Bge | Black | Blk-Blu |

Interior Codes: Blk/V=std; Blk/L=402; R/V=407; R/L=408; BB/V=414; BB/L=415; S/V=420; S/L=421; Sil/V=426; Sil/L=427; WB/V=450; G/V=430; Blu/V=418; Blu/L=419.

ABBREVIATIONS: Blk = Black, R = Red, W = White, S = Saddle, Blu = Blue, BB = Bright Blue, WB = White-Blue, Bge = Beige, Sil = Silver, G = Green, L=Leather, V=Vinyl

# 1967 CORVETTE

Production: 8,504 coupe, 14,436 convertible

## 1967 SERIAL NUMBERS

Body and Chassis: 194677S100001 through 194677S122940
(For coupes, first 6 digits are: 194377)

Engine Suffix: HE: Manual (327)
HH: A.I.R. (327)
HR: Automatic/A.I.R. (327)
HD: SHP/A.I.R. (327)
HO: Automatic (327)
HT: SHP (327)
HP: Power Steering, AC (327)
KH: SHP/AC/A.I.R. (327)
IL: Manual (427)
JC: Tri-Carb (427)
JE: SHP/Tri-Carb (427)

IT: Heavy Duty (427)
IU: Aluminum Heads (427)
IM: A.I.R. (427)
JF: A.I.R./Tri-Carb (427)
JH: A.I.R./AH (427)
IQ: Automatic (427)
JD: Automatic/Tri-Carb (427)
IR: A.I.R./Automatic (427)
JG: A.I.R./Auto/Tri-Carb (427)
JA: A.I.R./SHP/Tri-Carb (427)

A.I.R. = Air Injector Reactor (California), HP = High Performance, SHP = Special High Performance, AC = Air Conditioning, AH = Aluminum Heads

Distributor: 1111117, 1111194 (300 HP)      1111240 (430 HP)
1111196, 1111157 (350 HP)      1111258 (435 HP)
1111247, 1111294 (390, 400 HP)

Block Casting: 3892657 (300, 350 HP)      3869942 ( early 390, 400 HP)
3904351 (all 427)

Carburetor: Holley R3810A, R3814A (300, 350 HP)
Holley R3811A, R3815A (390 HP)
Holley R3660A, R3659A (400, 435 HP)
Holley R3888A, R3659A, R3418A (430, 400 HP/Automatic)

Head Casting: All 327 CI

## 1967 FACTS

● The 1967 model has similar styling to earlier Sting Rays but is devoid of much exterior trim. Emblems were removed from the standard hood and fenders. Fender vents continued functional, but were restyled as five angled slot vents, replacing the earlier three.

● The interior of the 1967 model was revamped with new seats. The parking brake handle was moved between the seats, the first year not located under the dash. Inner door panels are similar, but the lock buttons are located further forward and an attaching screw was added at the rear.

● Due to safety regulations, the knock-off wheel option was no longer available. For 1967, this option changed to a bolt-on style, cast alloy wheel. A central cap concealed the lug nuts.

● The standard wheel in 1967 was the rally wheel, the first time Corvettes came factory equipped with other than a single wheel cover assembly. Also, the wheel width for 1967 increased from 5½" to 6".

● 1967 is the first year of availability for the vinyl covering for optional hardtops.

# 1967 OPTIONS

| RPO # | DESCRIPTION | UNITS* | RETAIL $ |
|-------|-------------|--------|----------|
| 19437 | Base Corvette Sport Coupe | 8504 | $4388.75 |
| 19467 | Base Corvette Convertible | 14436 | 4240.75 |
| — | Genuine Leather Seats | 1601 | 79.00 |
| A01 | Soft Ray Tinted Glass, All Windows | 11331 | 15.80 |
| A02 | Soft Ray Tinted Glass, Windshield Only | 6558 | 10.55 |
| A31 | Electric Power Windows | 4036 | 57.95 |
| A82 | Headrests | 1762 | 42.15 |
| A85 | Shoulder Belts (coupe only) | 1426 | 26.35 |
| C07 | Auxiliary Hardtop (for roadster) | 6880 | 231.75 |
| C08 | Vinyl Covering for Auxiliary Hardtop | 1966 | 52.70 |
| C48 | Heater and Defroster Deletion (credit) | 35 | −97.85 |
| C60 | Air Conditioning | 3788 | 412.90 |
| F41 | Special Front and Rear Suspension | 2198 | 36.90 |
| G81 | Positraction Rear Axle, all ratios | 20,308 | 42.15 |
| J50 | Power Brakes | 4766 | 42.15 |
| J56 | Special Heavy Duty Brakes | 267 | 342.30 |
| K66 | Transistor Ignition System | 5759 | 73.75 |
| L36 | Optional 390 HP, 427 CI Engine | 5933 | 200.15 |
| L68 | Optional 400 HP, 427 CI Engine | 2101 | 305.50 |
| L71 | Optional 435 HP, 427 CI Engine | 3754 | 437.10 |
| L79 | Optional 350 HP, 327 CI Engine | 6375 | 105.35 |
| L88 | Optional 430 HP, 427 CI Engine | 20 | 947.90 |
| L89 | Aluminum Cylinder Heads for L71 | 16 | 368.65 |
| M20 | 4-Speed Transmission | 9157 | 184.35 |
| M21 | 4-Speed Close Ratio Transmission | 11015 | 184.35 |
| M22 | 4-Speed Close Ratio Trans., Heavy Duty | 20 | 237.00 |
| M35 | Powerglide Automatic Transmission | 2324 | 194.35 |
| N03 | 36 Gallon Fuel Tank (coupe only) | 2 | 198.05 |
| N11 | Off Road Exhaust System | 2326 | 36.90 |
| N14 | Side Mount Exhaust System | 4209 | 131.65 |
| N36 | Telescopic Steering Column | 2415 | 42.15 |
| N40 | Power Steering | 5747 | 94.80 |
| N89 | Special Cast Aluminum Bolt-On Wheels | 720 | 263.30 |
| P92 | Whitewall Tires, 7.75x15 | 13445 | 31.35 |
| QB1 | Redline Tires, 7.75x15 | 4320 | 46.65 |
| U15 | Speed Warning Indicator | 2108 | 10.55 |
| U69 | AM-FM Radio | 22193 | 172.75 |

# 1967 COLORS

| CODE | EXTERIOR | SOFT TOP | WHEELS | INTERIORS GM SUGGESTED |
|------|----------|----------|--------|------------------------|
| 900 | Tuxedo Black | Blk-W-TB | Silver | ( Blk-R-BB-S ) |
| 972 | Ermine White | Blk-W-TB | Silver | ( W-TB-G ) |
| 980 | Elkhart Blue | Blk-W-TB | Silver | Blk-TB |
| 977 | Lynndale Blue | Blk-W-TB | Silver | Blk-W-TB |
| 976 | Marina Blue | Blk-W-TB | Silver | Blk-BB-W |
| 983 | Goodwood Green | Blk-W-TB | Silver | Blk-S-W-G |
| 974 | Rally Red | Blk-W-TB | Silver | Blk-R-W |
| 986 | Silver Pearl | Blk-W-TB | Silver | Blk-TB |
| 984 | Sunfire Yellow | Blk-W-TB | Silver | Blk-W |
| 988 | Marlboro Maroon | Blk-W-TB | Silver | Blk-W-S |

**Interior Codes:** Blk/V=std; Blk/L=402; R/V=407; R/L=408; BB/V=414; BB/L=415; S/V=420; S/L=421; W/Blk/V=455; W/Blu/V=450; G/V=430; TB/V=418; TB/L=419.

ABBREVIATIONS: Blk = Black, R = Red, S = Saddle, G = Green, TB = Teal Blue, BB = Bright Blue, W = White/Black & White/Blue, L= Leather, V= Vinyl

# 1968 CORVETTE

Production: 9,936 coupe, 18,630 convertible

## 1968 SERIAL NUMBERS

Body and Chassis: 194678S400001 through 194678S428566
(For coupes, first 6 digits are 194378)

Engine Suffix: HE: Manual (327)                IM: HP/Tri-Carb (427)
HO: Automatic (327)             IO: HP/Auto/Tri-Carb (427)
HP: Power Steering/AC (327)     IQ: Automatic (427)
HT: SHP (327)                   IR: SHP/Tri-Carb (427)
IL: HP (427)                    IT: Heavy Duty
IU: SHP/Tri-Carb/AH (427)

SHP = Special High Performance, HP = High Performance, AH = Alu Heads.

## 1968 FACTS

• The 1968 Corvette features a completely new exterior and interior. The wheelbase is the same as previous Sting Rays, and the chassis components remain much the same. For the first time, the coupe model features removable roof panels and a removable rear window.

• Stylists kept the hidden headlight treatment on the 1968 model, but the units in the 1968 model "pop up" rather than revolve into position. Also, the 1968 units are vacuum operated, replacing the electrical systems of previous years.

• The 1968 interior has considerably less room than previous years, and the seats are set at much more severe rake angles creating a semi-reclining seating position. A light monitoring system was standard and utilized fiber optics to display functioning lights on a central console panel.

• The wheel rim width for 1968 was increased from 6" to 7". An increase again the following year to 8" makes the 1968 the only year with 7" rims.

• Engineers moved the battery from the engine compartment to a new stowage area behind the seats in 1968. The change was made because of the difficulty of reaching the battery in previous years in the engine area, but an advantage was realized in slightly better front to rear weight distribution.

• 1968 is the first year for use of the 3-speed automatic, the Turbohydramatic.

• 1968 models have unique door opening mechanisms. This year has a finger depression plate and a door button. In later years, the button was eliminated and the opening was activated by the depression plate.

• The windshield wipers of the 1968 model are hidden under a vacuum operated panel, a styling feature that proved to be somewhat troublesome in actual use.

• 1968 is the first year for elimination of side vent windows in the Corvette.

• 1968 is the last Corvette to have the ignition switch on the dash.

• 1968 Corvettes have four vertical front fender engine ducts. They are open and functional. There is no model identification above the vents as in the following year.

# 1968 OPTIONS

| RPO # | DESCRIPTION | UNITS* | RETAIL $ |
|---|---|---|---|
| 19437 | Base Corvette Sport Coupe | 9936 | 4663.00 |
| 19467 | Base Corvette Convertible | 18630 | 4320.00 |
| — | Genuine Leather Seat Trim | 2429 | 79.00 |
| A01 | Soft Ray Tinted Glass, All Windows | 17635 | 15.80 |
| A31 | Electric Power Windows | 7065 | 57.95 |
| A82 | Head Restraints | 3197 | 42.15 |
| A85 | Custom Shoulder Belts | 350 | 26.35 |
| C07 | Auxiliary Hardtop (for roadster) | 8735 | 231.75 |
| C08 | Vinyl Covering For Auxiliary Hardtop | 3050 | 52.70 |
| C50 | Rear Window Defroster | 693 | 31.60 |
| C60 | Air Conditioning | 5664 | 412.90 |
| F41 | Special Front and Rear Suspension | 1758 | 36.90 |
| G81 | Positraction Rear Axle, All Ratios | 27008 | 46.35 |
| J50 | Power Brakes | 9559 | 42.15 |
| J56 | Heavy Duty Brakes | 81 | 384.45 |
| K66 | Transistor Ignition System | 5457 | 73.75 |
| L36 | Optional 390 HP, 427 CI Engine | 7717 | 200.15 |
| L68 | Optional 400 HP, 427 CI Engine | 1932 | 305.50 |
| L71 | Optional 435 HP, 427 CI Engine | 2898 | 437.10 |
| L79 | Optional 350 HP, 327 CI Engine | 9440 | 105.35 |
| L88 | Optional 435 HP, 427 CI Engine | 80 | 947.90 |
| L71/89 | Optional 435 HP, 427 CI Engine | 624 | 805.75 |
| M20 | 4-Speed Transmission | 10760 | 184.35 |
| M21 | 4-Speed Close Ratio Transmission | 12337 | 184.35 |
| M22 | 4-Speed Close Ratio Trans., Heavy Duty | 80 | 263.30 |
| M40 | Turbo Hydramatic Automatic Transmission | 5063 | 226.45 |
| N11 | Off Road Exhaust System | 4695 | 36.90 |
| N36 | Telescopic Steering Column | 6477 | 42.15 |
| N40 | Power Steering | 12364 | 94.80 |
| P01 | Bright Metal Wheel Cover | 8971 | 57.95 |
| PT6 | Red Stripe Nylon Tires, F70x15 | 11686 | 31.30 |
| PT7 | White Stripe Nylon Tires, F70x15 | 9692 | 31.30 |
| UA6 | Alarm System | 388 | 26.35 |
| U15 | Speed Warning Indicator | 3453 | 10.55 |
| U69 | AM-FM Radio | 27920 | 172.75 |
| U79 | AM-FM Stereo Radio | 3311 | 278.10 |

*Sales during production year according to Chevrolet records.

# 1968 COLORS

| CODE | EXTERIOR | SOFT TOP | WHEELS | INTERIORS GM SUGGESTED |
|---|---|---|---|---|
| 900 | Tuxedo Black | Blk-W-Bge | Silver | ⎛ Blk-R-MB-DB ⎞ |
| 972 | Polar White | Blk-W-Bge | Silver | ⎝ DO-Tob-Gun ⎠ |
| 992 | Corvette Bronze | Blk-W-Bge | Silver | Blk-DO-Tob |
| 976 | LeMans Blue | Blk-W-Bge | Silver | Blk-MB-DB |
| 978 | International Blue | Blk-W-Bge | Silver | Blk-MB-DB |
| 988 | Cordovan Maroon | Blk-W-Bge | Silver | Blk |
| 974 | Rally Red | Blk-W-Bge | Silver | Blk-R |
| 986 | Silverstone Silver | Blk-W-Bge | Silver | Blk-DB-GM |
| 983 | British Green | Blk-W-Bge | Silver | Blk |
| 984 | Safari Yellow | Blk-W-Bge | Silver | Blk |

**Interior Codes:** Blk/V=std; Blk/L=402; R/V=407; R/L=408; MB/V=414; MB/L=415; DB/V=411; DO/V=425; DO/L=426; Tob/V=435; Tob/L=436; Gun/V=442.   **ABBREVIATIONS:** Blk = Black, R = Red, MB = Medium Blue, DB = Dark Blue, DO = Dark Orange, Gun = Gunmetal, W = White, Bge = Beige, Tob = Tobacco, L=Leather, V=Vinyl

# 1969 CORVETTE

Production: 22,129 coupe, 16,633 convertible

## 1969 SERIAL NUMBERS

Body and Chassis: 194679S700001 through 194679S738762
(For coupes, first 6 digits are: 194379)

Engine Suffix: HW: HP (350
HX: HP/AC (350)
HY: Manual (350)
HZ: Automatic (350)
LL: Automatic (427)
LM: HP (427)
LN: HP/Tri-Carb/Auto (427)
LO&IT: Heavy Duty (427)

LP: Aluminum Heads (427)
LQ: Tri-Carb/HP (427)
LR: Tri-Carb/SHP (427)
LT: Tri-Carb/SHP/HDC (427)
LU: Alum Heads/HDC (427)
LV: HD/Automatic (427)
LW: Alum Heads, Auto (427)
LX: Tri-Carb/SHP/Auto (427)

HP = High Performance, AC = Air Conditioning, SHP = Special High Performance, HDC = Heavy Duty Clutch.

## 1969 FACTS

• The 1969 Corvette body is very close in styling to the 1968 model. One apparent external change is the addition of the "Stingray" script above the front fender side louvers. The 1968 model was devoid of any side trim identification or markings.

• The outside door handle was changed on the 1969 model to the type used for several following years. The door opening mechanism was incorporated into what was strictly a finger depression grip in the 1968. The depression button used in 1968 was eliminated entirely and replaced with a near-flush key lock.

• 1969 is the first year for use of the 350 CI engine. This replaced the 327 CI engine line which had been used since 1962. These were not "all-new" engines, but simply the new generation of small block V-8 Chevy engines derived from the original V-8 introduced in 1955. External appearance is very similar to previous small blocks.

• 1969 is the first year for use of 8" wide wheel rims.

• In 1969, stylists incorporated the back-up lights into the inboard taillamps. This was a return to the system used in 1966. A single lamp above the license was used in 1967. In 1968, the lamps were under the bumpers.

• 1969 is the first Corvette to feature the steering column ignition lock. The system was designed to be an anti-theft device. It locked the steering shaft in place when the key was removed and made "hot starting" more difficult.

• The steering wheel in the 1969 model was reduced in diameter from 16" to 15".

• Map pockets were added to the passenger side dash area in 1969.

• 1969 is the first year for use of the headlight washer system.

• Trim louvers were available in 1969 to dress up the side fender vents. 1969 was the last year for the four vertical fender vent slots.

# 1969 OPTIONS

| RPO # | DESCRIPTION | UNITS* | RETAIL $ |
|-------|-------------|--------|----------|
| 19437 | Base Corvette Sport Coupe | 22129 | $4780.95 |
| 19467 | Base Corvette Convertible | 16633 | 4437.95 |
| — | Genuine Leather Seat Trim | 3729 | 79.00 |
| A01 | Soft Ray Tinted Glass, All Windows | 31270 | 16.90 |
| A31 | Electric Power Windows | 9816 | 63.20 |
| A85 | Custom Shoulder Belts | 600 | 42.15 |
| C07 | Auxiliary Hardtop (for roadster) | 7878 | 252.80 |
| C08 | Vinyl Covering for Auxiliary Hardtop | 3266 | 57.95 |
| C50 | Rear Window Defroster | 2485 | 32.65 |
| C60 | Air Conditioning | 11859 | 428.70 |
| F41 | Special Front and Rear Suspension | 1661 | 36.90 |
| — | Positraction Rear Axle, All Ratios | 36965 | 46.35 |
| J50 | Power Brakes | 16876 | 42.15 |
| K05 | Engine Block Heater | 824 | 10.55 |
| K66 | Transistor Ignition System | 5702 | 81.10 |
| L36 | Optional 390 HP, 427 CI Engine | 10531 | 221.20 |
| L46 | Optional 350 HP, 350 CI Engine | 12846 | 131.65 |
| L68 | Optional 400 HP, 427 CI Engine | 2072 | 326.55 |
| L71 | Optional 435 HP, 427 CI Engine | 2722 | 437.10 |
| L88 | Optional 435 HP, 427 CI Engine | 116 | 1032.15 |
| L89 | Optional 435 HP, 427 CI Engine | 390 | 832.05 |
| ZL1 | Optional Special 427 CI Engine | 2 | 3000.00 |
| M20 | 4-Speed Transmission | 16507 | 184.80 |
| M21 | 4-Speed Close Ratio Transmission | 13741 | 184.80 |
| M22 | 4-Speed Close Ratio Trans., Heavy Duty | 101 | 290.40 |
| M40 | Turbo Hydramatic Automatic Transmission | 8161 | 221.80 |
| N14 | Side Mount Exhaust System | 4355 | 147.45 |
| N37 | Tilt-Telescopic Steering Column | 10325 | 84.30 |
| N40 | Power Steering | 22866 | 105.35 |
| PT6 / PT7 | Red Stripe / White Stripe Nylon Tires | 26589 | 31.30 |
| TJ2 | Front Fender Louver Trim | 11962 | 21.10 |
| UA6 | Alarm System | 12436 | 26.35 |
| U15 | Speed Warning Indicator | 3561 | 11.60 |
| U69 | AM-FM Radio | 37985 | 172.75 |
| U79 | AM-FM Stereo Radio | 4114 | 278.10 |

*Sales during production year according to Chevrolet records.

# 1969 COLORS

| CODE | EXTERIOR | SOFT TOP | WHEELS | INTERIORS GM SUGGESTED |
|------|----------|----------|--------|------------------------|
| 900 | Tuxedo Black | Blk-W-Bge | Silver | Blk-BB-G-R-Gun-S |
| 972 | Can-Am White | Blk-W-Bge | Silver | Blk-BB-G-R-Gun-S |
| 974 | Monza Red | Blk-W-Bge | Silver | Blk-R-S |
| 976 | LeMans Blue | Blk-W-Bge | Silver | Blk-BB |
| 990 | Monaco Orange | Blk-W-Bge | Silver | Blk |
| 983 | Fathom Green | Blk-W-Bge | Silver | Blk-G-S |
| 984 | Daytona Yellow | Blk-W-Bge | Silver | Blk |
| 986 | Cortez Silver | Blk-W-Bge | Silver | Blk-BB-G-R-Gun-S |
| 988 | Burgundy | Blk-W-Bge | Silver | Blk-S |
| 980 | Riverside Gold | Blk-W-Bge | Silver | Blk |

**Interior Codes:** Blk/V=std; Blk/L=402; R/V=407; R/L=408; BB/V=411; BB/L=412; G/V=427; G/L=428; S/V=420; S/L=421; G/V=416; G/L=417.

ABBREVIATIONS: Blk = Black, R = Red, BB = Bright Blue, G = Green, S = Saddle, Gun = Gunmetal, W = White, Bge = Beige, L=Leather, V=Vinyl

# 1970 CORVETTE

Production: 10,668 coupe, 6,648 convertible

## 1970 SERIAL NUMBERS

**Body and Chassis:** 194670S400001 through 194670S417316
(For coupes, first 6 digits are 194370)

Engine
Suffix:

| | |
|---|---|
| CTL&CTD: Manual (350) | CTU: SHP/T-Ign (350) |
| CTM&CTG: Automatic (350) | CTV&CTK: SHP/T-Ign/Manual (350) |
| CTN&CTJ&CTH: HP (350) | CGW: HP/Auto (454) |
| CTO&CTJ: HP/AC (350) | CZU: HP (454) |
| CTP: HP/T-Ign (350) | CZL: HD (454) |
| CTQ: HP/T-Ign/AC (350) | CZN: HD/Auto (454) |
| CTR: SHP (350) | CRI: HP/T-Ign (454) |

HP = High Performance, T-Ign = Transistor Ignition, AC = Air Conditioning,
SHP = Special High Performance, HD = Heavy Duty.

## 1970 FACTS

● The body of the 1970 model Corvette was considerably updated. Fiberglass side body shapes were altered to create fender flares behind the wheels to minimize damage to the body by debris thrown by the wheels, a problem common to 1968 and 1969 models. A new style side fender louver replaced the four vertical slots of the previous two years.

● 1970 is the first year for the availability of the deluxe interior option. This includes not only leather seats, but other deluxe appointments such as wood grain on the console and door panel areas and special carpet treatment.

● The interior of the 1970 features subtle refinements. The seats were redesigned for additional headroom and for easier release for access to the storage area. The shoulder belt retractor containers were redesigned and relocated for a bit of additional storage room behind the seats.

● In 1970, tinted glass, 4-speed transmission (or automatic) and positraction became standard equipment.

● The 427 CI engine was increased in size to 454 CI for the 1970 model. The small block remained at 350 CI, but a new engine was added to the lineup, a solid lifter small block with the now immortal designation of LT-1. This was the first solid lifter Corvette small block available since 1965. For the 1970 model, Chevrolet announced a strong new 454 CI engine with an aluminum block, the LS-7. Although the engines were built and sold to racing enterprises, and most option sheets list the engine's availability, none were ever installed in production Corvettes. The horsepower rating was 460, and the projected cost in the neighborhood of $3000.00.

● Because of its late introduction in February, 1970, the 1970 model Corvette had the lowest production since 1962. 17,316 1970 models were made.

● The 1970 model was given a new square mesh grill with amber-bulb, clear lens turn signals mounted at the extreme corners of the grill. New exhaust exits were also designed for the 1970 model, being square in shape to replace the round exits of previous years.

# 1970 OPTIONS

| RPO # | DESCRIPTION | UNITS* | RETAIL $ |
|-------|-------------|--------|----------|
| 19437 | Base Corvette Sport Coupe | 10668 | 5192.00 |
| 19467 | Base Corvette Convertible | 6648 | 4849.00 |
| — | Custom Interior Trim | 3191 | 158.00 |
| A31 | Electric Power Windows | 4813 | 63.20 |
| A85 | Custom Shoulder Belts | 475 | 42.15 |
| C07 | Auxiliary Hardtop (for roadster) | 2556 | 273.85 |
| C08 | Vinyl Covering for Auxiliary Hardtop | 832 | 63.20 |
| C50 | Rear Window Defroster | 1281 | 36.90 |
| C60 | Air Conditioning | 6659 | 447.65 |
| — | Positraction Axle, Optional Ratio | 2862 | 12.65 |
| J50 | Power Brakes | 8984 | 47.40 |
| L46 | Optional 350 HP, 350 CI Engine | 4910 | 158.00 |
| LS5 | Optional 390 HP, 454 CI Engine | 4473 | 289.65 |
| LS7 | Optional 460 HP, 454 CI Engine | - | * |
| LT1 | Optional 370 HP, 350 CI Engine | 1287 | 447.60 |
| M21 | 4-Speed Close Ratio Transmission | 4383 | nc |
| M22 | 4-Speed Close Ratio Trans., Heavy Duty | 25 | 95.00 |
| M40 | Turbo Hydramatic Automatic Transmission | 5102 | nc |
| N37 | Tilt-Telescopic Steering Column | 5803 | 84.30 |
| N40 | Power Steering | 11907 | 105.35 |
| P01 | Custom Wheel Covers | 3467 | 57.95 |
| PT7 | White Stripe Nylon Tires, F70x15 | 6589 | 31.30 |
| PU9 | White Letter Nylon Tires, F70x15 | 7985 | 33.15 |
| T60 | Heavy Duty Battery | 165 | 15.80 |
| UA6 | Alarm System | 6727 | 31.60 |
| U69 | AM-FM Radio | 16991 | 172.75 |
| U79 | AM-FM Stereo Radio | 2462 | 278.10 |

*Sales during production year according to Chevrolet records.

*The LS7 engine was never installed in production Corvettes. The projected cost was approximately $3000.00.

• Option list does not include additional items available as dealer installed accessories.

# 1970 COLORS

| CODE | EXTERIOR | SOFT TOP | WHEELS | INTERIORS GM SUGGESTED |
|------|----------|----------|--------|------------------------|
| 976 | Mulsanne Blue | Blk-W | Silver | Blk-Blu |
| 979 | Bridgehampton Blue | Blk-W | Silver | Blk-Blu |
| 982 | Donnybrooke Green | Blk-W | Silver | Blk-Br-G-S |
| 992 | Laguna Gray | Blk-W | Silver | Blk-Blu-Br-G-R-S |
| 975 | Marlboro Maroon | Blk-W | Silver | Blk-Br-S |
| 993 | Corvette Bronze | Blk-W | Silver | Blk |
| 974 | Monza Red | Blk-W | Silver | Blk-Br-R-S |
| 986 | Cortez Silver | Blk-W | Silver | Blk-Blu-Br-G-R-S |
| 972 | Classic White | Blk-W | Silver | Blk-Blu-Br-G-R-S |
| 984 | Daytona Yellow | Blk-W | Silver | Blk-G |

Interior Codes: Blk/V=std; Blk/L=402; R/V=407; Blu/V=411; S/V=418; S/L=424; Br/V=414; G/V=422.

ABBREVIATIONS: Blk = Black, Blu = Blue, Br = Brown, R = Red, G = Green, S = Saddle, W = White, L=Leather, V=Vinyl

• Only Black and Saddle were available in leather.

# 1971 CORVETTE

Production: 14,680 coupe, 7,121 convertible

## 1971 SERIAL NUMBERS

**Body and Chassis:** 194671S100001 through 194671S121801
(For coupes, first 6 digits are 194371)

**Engine Suffix:** CJL: 270 HP, 350 CI, 4-Speed Transmission
CGT&CJK: 270 HP, 350 CI, Turbohydramatic 400
CGZ: 330 HP, 350 CI, 4-Speed Transmission
CGY: 330 HP, 350 CI, HD 4-Speed Transmission
CPJ: 365 HP, 454 CI, Turbohydramatic 400
CPH: 365 HP, 454 CI, 4-Speed Transmission
CPW: 425 HP, 454 CI, 4-Speed Transmission
CPX: 425 HP, 454 CI, Turbohydramatic 400

## 1971 FACTS

● The 1971 is almost a duplicate of the 1970 model. These two Corvette years are the most similar since the 1956-57 and 1959-60 models. Two reasons are generally given for the lack of change. First, the 1970 model was introduced almost five months late, as a result of a decision to extend 1969 production which itself was delayed initially due to labor disputes. Because of the short 1970 model run, GM management apparently felt that an extensive 1971 model change was unnecessary. The second reason often cited is that a GM mandate to its divisions to reduce octane requirements for the 1971 models kept engineers too busy to worry about appearance changes.

● The 1971 was the last Corvette model to have the fiber-optics light monitoring system. This was dropped to offset the cost of the anti-theft alarm system made standard for the 1972 model.

● The 1971 engines available were variations of the 350 CI and 454 CI engines of the previous year. The 1970 to 1971 transition was the first really major horsepower drop across-the-board due to emissions considerations. This occurred due to the GM mandated reduction of octane requirements to 91 Research Octane for the eventual switch to no-lead fuels. Although the no-lead was required for catalytic converters which were not to appear on Corvettes until 1975, GM made the switch early to allow fuel companies to start marketing their low and no-lead fuels.

● Aluminum heads were available in the LS-6, an expensive successor to the never available-for-street-use LS-7, 454 CI engine.

● In 1971, a ZR1 factory racing option was available. It included the LT-1 engine, HD 4-speed, HD power brakes, aluminum radiator, special springs and shocks, special front stabilizer, and rear wheel spindle strut shafts. A ZR1 could not be ordered with power windows, power steering, air conditioning, rear window defroster, wheel covers or radio.

● Except for very early cars with clear parking light lens, all others were amber.

## 1971 OPTIONS

| RPO # | DESCRIPTION | UNITS* | RETAIL $ |
|-------|-------------|--------|----------|
| 19437 | Base Corvette Sport Coupe | 14680 | 5496.00 |
| 19467 | Base Corvette Convertible | 7121 | 5259.00 |
| — | Custom Interior Trim | 2602 | 158.00 |
| A31 | Electric Power Windows | 6192 | 79.00 |
| A85 | Custom Shoulder Belts | 677 | 42.00 |
| C07 | Auxiliary Hardtop (for roadster) | 2619 | 274.00 |
| C08 | Vinyl Covering for Auxiliary Hardtop | 832 | 63.00 |
| C50 | Rear Window Defroster | 1598 | 42.00 |
| C60 | Air Conditioning | 11481 | 459.00 |
| — | Positraction Axle, Optional Ratio | 2395 | 13.00 |
| J50 | Power Brakes | 13558 | 47.00 |
| LS5 | Optional 365 HP, 454 CI Engine | 5097 | 295.00 |
| LS6 | Optional 425 HP, 454 CI Engine | 188 | 1221.00 |
| LT1 | Optional 330 HP, 350 CI Engine | 1949 | 483.00 |
| ZR1 | Optional 330 HP, 350 CI Engine | 8 | 1010.00 |
| ZR2 | Optional 425 HP, 454 CI Engine | 12 | 1747.00 |
| M21 | 4-Speed Close Ratio Transmission | 2387 | nc |
| M22 | 4-Speed Close Ratio Trans., Heavy Duty | 130 | 100.00 |
| M40 | Turbo Hydramatic Automatic Transmission | 10060 | nc |
| N37 | Tilt-Telescopic Steering Column | 8130 | 84.30 |
| N40 | Power Steering | 17904 | 115.90 |
| P02 | Wheel Covers | 3007 | 63.00 |
| PT7 | White Stripe Nylon Tires, F70x15 | 6711 | 28.00 |
| PU9 | White Lettered Nylon Tires, F70x15 | 12449 | 42.00 |
| T60 | Heavy Duty Battery | 1455 | 15.80 |
| U69 | AM-FM Radio | 21509 | 178.00 |
| U79 | AM-FM Stereo Radio | 3431 | 283.00 |

*Sales during production year according to Chevrolet records.

• The cost of the M40 Automatic Transmission with available high performance engines was $100.00.

## 1971 COLORS

| CODE | EXTERIOR | SOFT TOP | WHEELS | INTERIORS GM SUGGESTED |
|------|----------|----------|--------|------------------------|
| 976 | Mulsanne Blue | Blk-W | Silver | Blk-DB |
| 979 | Bridgehampton Blue | Blk-W | Silver | Blk-DB |
| 983 | Brands Hatch Green | Blk-W | Silver | Blk-DG |
| 988 | Steel Cities Gray | Blk-W | Silver | Blk-S |
| 987 | Ontario Orange | Blk-W | Silver | Blk-DG-S |
| 973 | Mille Miglia Red | Blk-W | Silver | Blk-R |
| 905 | Nevada Silver | Blk-W | Silver | Blk-DB-DG-R |
| 972 | Classic White | Blk-W | Silver | Blk-DB-DG-R-S |
| 912 | Sunflower Yellow | Blk-W | Silver | Blk-DG-S |
| 989 | War Bonnet Yellow | Blk-W | Silver | Blk-DG-S |

**Interior Codes:** Blk/V=Std; Blk/L=402; R/V=407; DB/V=412; S/V=417; S/L=420; DG/V=423.

ABBREVIATIONS: Blk = Black, DB = Dark Blue, S = Saddle, W = White, R = Red, DG = Dark Green, L=Leather, V=Vinyl

• Some 1971 models may have two-digit paint codes in order as above: 26, 27, 48, 98, 97, 76, 13, 10, 52, 91.

• Only Black and Saddle were available in leather.

# 1972 CORVETTE

Production: 20,496 coupe, 6,508 convertible

## 1972 SERIAL NUMBERS

Body and Chassis: 1Z67K2S500001 through 1Z67K2S527004
- 3rd and 4th digits are 37 for coupes
- 5th digit varies as follows: K = Base
  L = LT-1
  V,W = 454 CI

Engine Suffix: CKW: 4-Spd (350)
CDH: 4-Spd/NB2 (350)
CKX: Auto (350)
CDJ: Auto/NB2 (350)
CKY: 4-Spd/LT-1 (350)
CKZ: HD 4-Spd/LT-1 (350)

CRT: 4-Spd/LT-1/AR (350)
CPH: 4-Spd (454)
CPJ: Auto (454)
CSR: AR (454)
CSS: AR (454)

Auto = Turbohydramatic, HD = Heavy Duty, AR = Air Injector Reactor, NB2 = California Emissions.

## 1972 FACTS

• The 1972 model Corvette is externally very similar to the previous two model years. Although not unique in many respects, the 1972 model desirability stems from the fact that it marked the end of era for several Corvette design features.

• The 1972 Corvette is the last Corvette coupe to feature a removable rear window.

• The 1972 Corvette is the last to feature an egg crate grill.

• The 1972 Corvette is the last to feature side fender grills, though later models have functional fender vents.

• 1972 was the last year of availability for the LT-1 engine, a solid lifter small block.

• 1972 is the only year that the LT-1 could be factory ordered with air conditioning, and this was for only four months of production. The production quantity most often cited is 286. Chevrolet rarely offered air conditioning with solid lifter engines, since the higher revolutions attainable with mechanical valve lifters tends to spin air conditioning belts off their pulleys. Prior to 1972, the last Corvette available with the combination of solid lifter engine and air conditioning was the 1965 model equipped with the 365 HP engine.

• The 1972 model was the first Corvette to have the anti-theft alarm system as standard equipment.

• Significantly, the 1972 model is the last Corvette to have chrome protection at both front and rear, marking the end of a Corvette tradition since the first 1953 model.

48

# 1972 OPTIONS

| RPO # | DESCRIPTION | UNITS* | RETAIL $ |
|---|---|---|---|
| 19437 | Base Corvette Sport Coupe | 20496 | 5533.00 |
| 19467 | Base Corvette Convertible | 6508 | 5296.00 |
| — | Custom Interior Trim | 4572 | 158.00 |
| A31 | Electric Power Windows | 9495 | 85.35 |
| A85 | Custom Shoulder Belts | 749 | 26.35 |
| C07 | Auxiliary Hardtop (for roadster) | 2646 | 273.85 |
| C08 | Vinyl Roof Covering For Auxiliary Hardtop | 811 | 158.00 |
| C50 | Rear Window Defroster | 2221 | 42.15 |
| C60 | Air Conditioning | 17227 | 464.50 |
| — | Positraction Axle, Optional Ratio | 1986 | 12.65 |
| J50 | Power Brakes | 18770 | 47.40 |
| LS5 | Optional 270 HP, 454 CI Engine | 3913 | 294.90 |
| LT1 | Optional 255 HP, 350 CI Engine | 1741 | 483.45 |
| ZR1 | Optional 255 HP, 350 CI Engine | 20 | 1010.05 |
| M21 | 4-Speed Close Ratio Transmission | 1638 | nc |
| M40 | Turbo Hydramatic Transmission | 14543 | nc |
| N37 | Tilt-Telescopic Steering Column | 12992 | 84.30 |
| N40 | Power Steering | 23794 | 115.90 |
| PO2 | Custom Wheel Covers | 3593 | 63.20 |
| PT7 | White Stripe Nylon Tires, F70x15 | 6666 | 30.35 |
| PU9 | White Lettered Nylon Tires, F70x15 | 16623 | 43.65 |
| T60 | Heavy Duty Battery | 2969 | 15.80 |
| U69 | AM-FM Radio | 26669 | 178.00 |
| U79 | AM-FM Stereo Radio | 7189 | 283.35 |

*Sales during production year according to Chevrolet records.

● The cost of the M40 Automatic Transmission with available high performance engines was $97.00.

● LT-1/air cars came with a 5600 RPM tachometer. Normally, the LT-1 had a 6500 RPM tach, but the lower red line served to remind owners of air cars that the drive belts wouldn't sustain the higher revs without slipping off pulleys.

# 1972 COLORS

| CODE | EXTERIOR | SOFT TOP | WHEELS | INTERIORS GM SUGGESTED |
|---|---|---|---|---|
| 945 | Bryar Blue | Blk-W | Silver | Blk |
| 979 | Targa Blue | Blk-W | Silver | Blk-Blu |
| 988 | Steel Cities Gray | Blk-W | Silver | Blk-R-S |
| 946 | Elkhart Green | Blk-W | Silver | Blk-S |
| 987 | Ontario Orange | Blk-W | Silver | Blk-S |
| 973 | Mille Miglia Red | Blk-W | Silver | Blk-R-S |
| 924 | Pewter Silver | Blk-W | Silver | Blk-Blu-R-S |
| 972 | Classic White | Blk-W | Silver | Blk-Blu-R-S |
| 912 | Sunflower Yellow | Blk-W | Silver | Blk-S |
| 989 | War Bonnet Yellow | Blk-W | Silver | Blk-S |

**Interior Codes:** Blk/V=std; Blk/L=404; R/V=407; Blu/V=412; S/V=417; S/L=421.

ABBREVIATIONS: Blk = Black, Blu = Blue, W = White, R = Red, S = Saddle
L=Leather, V=Vinyl

● Only Black and Saddle were available in leather.

● Seat and shoulder belts matched interior except for the blue interior which got dark blue belts.

# 1973 CORVETTE

Production: 25,521 coupe, 4,943 convertible

## 1973 SERIAL NUMBERS

**Body and Chassis:** 1Z67J3S400001 through 1Z67J3S434464
- 3rd and 4th digits are 37 for coupes
- 5th digit varies as follows: J = Base  T = L-82  Z = 454

**Engine Suffix:** CKZ: L48/4-Spd (350)     CLD: L82/Auto (350)
CLA: L48/Auto (350)     CLH: L82/Auto/NB2 (350)
CLR: L82/4-Spd (350)     CWS: LS4/Auto/NB2 (454)
CLB: L48/4-Spd/NB2 (350)     CWT: LS4/4-Spd/NB2 (454)
CLC: L48/Auto/NB2 (350)     CWM: LS4/4-Spd (454)
CLS: L82/4-Spd/NB2 (350)     CWR: LS4/Auto (454)

Auto = Turbohydramatic, NB2 = California Emissions

## 1973 FACTS

• 1973 is the first model Corvette to have bumper systems designed to meet federal 5 mph standards. The 1973 rear was the same as 1972, but the front was redesigned with a body color bumper which added 35 lbs of weight, but which could survive 5 mph impacts without damage to the light or safety equipment.

• Noise reduction had a major impact on the design considerations of the 1973 model. For the first time since 1956, a solid lifter engine was no longer available in the Corvette. Sound deadening material was sprayed on many inner panels and new deadening pad was installed under the hood to muffle engine noise.

• The LT-1 engine was removed from the option list in 1973 and replaced by the L-82, a hydraulic lifter engine.

• The inner doors of the 1973 model have steel beams for greater side impact protection.

• New chassis mounts were designed for the 1973 model to better isolate road chatter and vibration. The new mounts are rubber with steel sleeves. The rubber gives vertical cushioning while the steel maintains stability.

• A new coolant recovery system was designed for the 1973 Corvette which permitted high temperature overflow coolant to be captured and returned to the radiator after cooling.

• The 1973 Corvette coupe was the first since 1967 to have a rear window which could not be removed. When this feature was removed, an additional two inches of luggage space height was gained since the tray for storing the window was also removed.

• The lifting windshield wiper door was deleted from 1973 models, but a new hood with rear cold air induction was introduced.

• A great deal of confusion exists regarding 1973 production because for some reason, 4000 serial numbers were never built. The last '73 Corvette's serial number ends with 34,464, but only 30,464 cars were built. The numbers somehow lost were 24001 through 28000.

# 1973 OPTIONS

| RPO # | DESCRIPTION | UNITS* | RETAIL $ |
|-------|-------------|--------|----------|
| 1YZ37 | Base Corvette Sport Coupe | 25521 | 5561.50 |
| 1YZ67 | Base Corvette Convertible | 4943 | 5398.50 |
| — | Custom Interior Trim | 13434 | 154.00 |
| A31 | Electric Power Windows | 14024 | 83.00 |
| A85 | Custom Shoulder Belts | 788 | 41.00 |
| C07 | Auxiliary Hardtop (for roadster) | 1328 | 267.00 |
| C08 | Vinyl Roof Covering for Auxiliary Hardtop | 323 | 62.00 |
| C50 | Rear Window Defroster | 4412 | 41.00 |
| C60 | Air Conditioning | 21578 | 452.00 |
| — | Positraction Axle, Optional Ratio | 1791 | 12.00 |
| J50 | Power Brakes | 24168 | 46.00 |
| L82 | Optional 250 HP, 350 CI Engine | 5710 | 299.00 |
| LS4 | Optional 275 HP, 454 CI Engine | 4412 | 250.00 |
| M21 | 4-Speed Close Ratio Transmission | 3704 | nc |
| M40 | Turbo Hydramatic Automatic Transmission | 17927 | nc |
| N37 | Tilt-Telescopic Steering Column | 17949 | 82.00 |
| N40 | Power Steering | 27872 | 113.00 |
| P02 | Custom Wheel Covers | 1739 | 62.00 |
| QRM | White Stripe Steel Belted Radial Tires, GR70x15 | 19903 | 32.00 |
| QRZ | White Letter Steel Belted Radial Tires, GR70x15 | 4541 | 45.00 |
| T60 | Heavy Duty Battery | 4912 | 15.00 |
| U58 | AM-FM Stereo Radio | 12482 | 276.00 |
| U69 | AM-FM Radio | 17598 | 173.00 |
| UF1 | Map Light | 8186 | 5.00 |
| YJ8 | Cast Aluminum Wheels | 4 | 175.00 |
| Z07 | Off Road Suspension and Brake Package | 45 | 369.00 |

*Sales during production year according to Chevrolet records.

● The YJ8 Cast Aluminum Wheel option was not actually available during 1973. Very early in production, Chevrolet rejected the wheels for quality reasons (they had been supplied by a California vendor) and recalled the wheels that had been released. Rumors place the number of wheels produced at 800 sets, and some of these are still at large.

# 1973 COLORS

| CODE | EXTERIOR | SOFT TOP | WHEELS | INTERIORS GM SUGGESTED |
|------|----------|----------|--------|------------------------|
| 922 | Medium Blue | Blk-W | Silver | Blk-MB-MS |
| 927 | Dark Blue | Blk-W | Silver | Blk-MB-DR-MS |
| 945 | Blue-Green | Blk-W | Silver | Blk-DR-DS-MS |
| 947 | Elkhart Green | Blk-W | Silver | Blk-MS |
| 980 | Orange | Blk-W | Silver | Blk-MS |
| 976 | Mille Miglia Red | Blk-W | Silver | Blk-MB-DR-DS-MS |
| 914 | Silver | Blk-W | Silver | Blk-MB-DR-DS-MS |
| 910 | Classic White | Blk-W | Silver | Blk-MB-DR-DS-MS |
| 952 | Yellow | Blk-W | Silver | Blk-MB-DS |
| 953 | Yellow (Metallic) | Blk-W | Silver | Blk-MB |

**Interior Codes:** Blk/V=400; Blk/L=404; MB/V=413; MS/V=415; MS/L=416; DS/V=418; DS/L=422; DR/V=425.

ABBREVIATIONS: Blk = Black, MB = Midnight Blue, MS = Medium Saddle, W = White, DR = Dark Red, DS = Dark Saddle, L=Leather, V=Vinyl

● Only Black, Dark Saddle and Medium Saddle were available in leather.

# 1974 CORVETTE

Production: 32,028 coupe, 5,474 convertible

## 1974 SERIAL NUMBERS

Body and Chassis: 1Z67J4S400001 through 1Z67J4S437502
- 3rd and 4th digits are 37 for coupes
- 5th digit varies as follows: J = Base
  - T = L-82
  - Z = 454

Engine Suffix:

| | |
|---|---|
| CKZ: L48/4-Spd (350) | CLD: L82/Auto (350) |
| CLA: L48/Auto (350) | CLS: L82/Auto/NB2(350) |
| CLR: L82/4-Spd (350) | CWS: LS4/Auto/NB2 (454) |
| CLB: L48-Spd/NB2 (350) | CWM: LS4/4-Spd (454) |
| CLC: L48/Auto/NB2 (350) | CWR: LS4/Auto (454) |
| CLH: L82/4-Spd/NB2(350) | CWT: LS4/4-Spd/NB2(454) |

Auto = Turbohydramatic, NB2 = California Emissions

## 1974 FACTS

- 1974 completed the transition to "soft" bumpers with the addition of the new body color rear bumper system. The outside of the bumper is urethane plastic with built in recesses for the license and taillights. Under the urethane is an aluminum impact bar mounted on two slider brackets. The urethane rear bumper on 1974 models is two-piece, with a seam running vertically up the middle. Later years have one-piece urethane covers.

- 1974 is the last Corvette to have genuine dual exhausts. It is also the last to have a non-catalytic exhaust. In later years, dual exhausts flow through a single catalytic converter, then split again into dual exhausts. Since it has no converter, the fuel requirement for the 1974 is 91 octane regular leaded. Later years with the converter require unleaded fuel.

- 1974 is the last year of availability for the 454 CI engine.

- The standard alarm system activator mechanism was moved from the rear panel to the driver side fender in 1974.

- 1974 models with power steering have special power steering pumps with magnets to attract floating metallic debris.

- The radiators in 1974 models were redesigned for more efficient cooling at low speeds.

- The shoulder belts on 1974 models are integrated with the lap belts. Also, the shoulder belt restraint system was changed in 1974. Previously, the belts permitted forward movement but locked when the forward pull exceeded a preset rate. The new system first installed in the 1974 model, contains a small swinging weight which locks the belts when the car decelerates quickly. Movement within the car is not restricted at all as long as the car itself is stable.

- The inside rear view mirror on the 1974 model was increased in width to 10".

# 1974 OPTIONS

| RPO # | DESCRIPTION | UNITS* | RETAIL $ |
|-------|-------------|--------|----------|
| 1YZ37 | Base Corvette Sport Coupe | 32028 | 6001.50 |
| 1YZ67 | Base Corvette Convertible | 5474 | 5765.50 |
| — | Custom Interior Trim | 19959 | 154.00 |
| A31 | Electric Power Windows | 23940 | 86.00 |
| A85 | Custom Shoulder Belts | 618 | 41.00 |
| C07 | Auxiliary Hardtop (for roadster) | 2612 | 267.00 |
| C08 | Vinyl Covered Auxiliary Hardtop | 367 | 329.00 |
| C50 | Rear Window Defroster | 9322 | 43.00 |
| C60 | Air Conditioning | 29397 | 467.00 |
| FE7 | Gymkhana Suspension | 1905 | 7.00 |
| — | Positraction Axle, Optional Ratio | 1219 | 12.00 |
| J50 | Power Brakes | 33306 | 49.00 |
| L82 | Optional 250 HP, 350 CI Engine | 6690 | 299.00 |
| LS4 | Optional 270 HP, 454 CI Engine | 3494 | 250.00 |
| M21 | 4-Speed Close Ratio Transmission | 3494 | nc |
| M40 | Turbo Hydramatic Automatic Transmission | 25146 | nc |
| N37 | Tilt-Telescopic Steering Column | 27700 | 82.00 |
| N41 | Power Steering | 35944 | 117.00 |
| QRM | White Stripe SBR Tires, GR70x15 | 9140 | 32.00 |
| QRZ | White Letter SBR Tires, GR70x15 | 24102 | 45.00 |
| U05 | Dual Horns | 5258 | 4.00 |
| U58 | AM-FM Stereo Radio | 19581 | 276.00 |
| U69 | AM-FM Radio | 17374 | 173.00 |
| UA1 | Heavy Duty Battery | 9169 | 15.00 |
| UF1 | Map Light | 16101 | 5.00 |
| Z07 | Off Road Suspension and Brake Package | 47 | 400.00 |

*Sales during production year according to Chevrolet records.

• The cost of the M40 Automatic Transmission with available high performance engines was $103.00.

• The FE7 Gymkhana Suspension package includes stiffer front anti-roll bar and stiffer springs. Not recommended for pleasure driving use only.

• Base prices include standard 350 CI, 195 HP engine.

# 1974 COLORS

| CODE | EXTERIOR | SOFT TOP | WHEELS | INTERIORS GM SUGGESTED |
|------|----------|----------|--------|------------------------|
| 922 | Corvette Med Blue | Blk-W | Silver | Blk-DB-Sil |
| 968 | Dark Brown | Blk-W | Silver | Blk-N-S-Sil |
| 917 | Corvette Gray | Blk-W | Silver | (Blk-DB-N- |
| 910 | Classic White | Blk-W | Silver | DR-S-Sil ) |
| 980 | Corvette Orange | Blk-W | Silver | Blk-N-S-Sil |
| 976 | Mille Miglia Red | Blk-W | Silver | Blk-N-DR-S-Sil |
| 974 | Medium Red | Blk-W | Silver | Blk-N-DR-S-Sil |
| 914 | Silver Mist | Blk-W | Silver | Blk-DB-DR-S-Sil |
| 948 | Dark Green | Blk-W | Silver | Blk-N-S-Sil |
| 956 | Bright Yellow | Blk-W | Silver | Blk-N-S-Sil |

**Interior Codes:** Blk/V=400; Blk/L=404; DB/V=413; Sil/V=406; Sil/L=407; N/V=408; S/V=415; S/L=416; DR/V=425.

ABBREVIATIONS: Blk = Black, DB = Dark Blue, Sil = Silver, N = Neutral, S = Saddle, DR = Dark Red, W = White, L=Leather, V=Vinyl

• Only Black, Saddle and Silver were available in leather.

# 1975 CORVETTE

Production: 33,836 coupe, 4,629 convertible

## 1975 SERIAL NUMBERS

Body and Chassis: 1Z67J5S400001 through 1Z67J5S438465

- 3rd and 4th digits are 37 for coupes
- 5th digit varies as follows: J = Base   T = L-82

Engine Suffix: CRJ: 4-Speed
CRK: Automatic
CRL: 4-Speed/HP
CRM: Automatic/HP
CHA: 4-Speed
CHB: Automatic w/fed
CHZ: Automatic w/calif

CUT: 4-Speed/HP
CUA: 4-Speed
CUB: 4-Speed
CUD: 4-Speed/HP
CHC: 4-Speed/HP
CHR: Automatic/HP w/calif
CKC: Automatic/HP w/fed

HP = High Performance (L-82)

## 1975 FACTS

● The soft bumpers were redesigned structurally in the 1975 model but external appearance of the car overall remained similar to the previous year. The front bumper was given an inner core of honeycomb plastic to better absorb impact. The exterior of the front bumper was changed slightly and simulated vertical "pads" were added. The rear bumper was redesigned internally to use shock absorber type struts to cushion impact. The exterior of the 1975 rear bumper was one-piece, replacing the two-piece 1974 design. "Pads" were also added to the rear and the 1975 bumper was designed with more side tuck to slim the appearance.

● 1975 is the first year for the use of the catalytic converter on a Corvette. A single converter was used and mounted just below the passenger side floor. Dual exhausts were routed into the converter then split again for dual exit.

● 1975 is the last year of production for the Corvette convertible. The last Corvette roadster was built during the last week of July, 1975. It was one of only 4,629 open Corvettes built during the 1975 model production.

● Engine availability in the 1975 Corvette dropped to the lowest number since 1955. In 1975, only the L-82 engine option was offered as a choice to the base L-48. With the deletion of the 454 CI engine, the 1975 Corvette became the first since the 1964 model to not offer a choice of displacement

● 1975 was the first model Corvette to have the HEI (High Energy Ignition) system. The HEI is quite different than the transistor ignition systems available on Corvettes for over 10 years and included the Corvette's first pointless distributor.

● The 1975 Corvette tachometer is electronically driven, a change mandated by the HEI system's new type of distributor.

● 1975 is the first year for the use of L-82 hood emblems.

● 1975 is the first year for a kilometer-per-hour subface on the speedometer.

● 1975 was the first Corvette model with a headlight warning buzzer and the last for Astro-ventilation.

# 1975 OPTIONS

| RPO # | DESCRIPTION | UNITS* | RETAIL $ |
|---|---|---|---|
| 1YZ37 | Base Corvette Sport Coupe | 33836 | 6810.10 |
| 1YZ67 | Base Corvette Convertible | 4629 | 6550.10 |
| — | Custom Interior Trim | - | 154.00 |
| A31 | Electric Power Windows | 28745 | 93.00 |
| A85 | Custom Shoulder Belts | 646 | 41.00 |
| C07 | Auxiliary Hardtop (for roadsters) | 2407 | 267.00 |
| C08 | Vinyl Covered Auxiliary Hardtop | 279 | 350.00 |
| C50 | Rear Window Defroster | 13760 | 46.00 |
| C60 | Air Conditioning | 31914 | 490.00 |
| FE7 | Gymkhana Suspension | 3194 | 7.00 |
| — | Positraction Axle, Optional Ratio | 1969 | 12.00 |
| J50 | Power Brakes | 35842 | 50.00 |
| L82 | Optional 205 HP, 350 CI Engine | 2372 | 336.00 |
| M21 | 4-Speed Close Ratio Transmission | 1057 | nc |
| M40 | Turbo Hydramatic Automatic Transmission | 28473 | nc |
| N37 | Tilt-Telescopic Steering Column | 31830 | 82.00 |
| N41 | Power Steering | 37591 | 129.00 |
| QRM | White Stripe SBR Tires, GR70x15 | 5233 | 35.00 |
| QRZ | White Letter SBR Tires, GR70x15 | 30407 | 48.00 |
| U05 | Dual Horns | 22011 | 4.00 |
| U58 | AM-FM Stereo Radio | 24701 | 284.00 |
| U69 | AM-FM Radio | 12902 | 178.00 |
| UA1 | Heavy Duty Battery | 16778 | 15.00 |
| UF1 | Map Light | 21676 | 5.00 |
| Z07 | Off Road Suspension and Brake Package | 144 | 400.00 |

*Sales during production year according to Chevrolet records.

• The cost of the M40 Automatic Transmission with the L-82 engine option was $120.00.

• Base prices include standard 350 CI, 165 HP engine.

# 1975 COLORS

| CODE | EXTERIOR | SOFT TOP | WHEELS | INTERIORS GM SUGGESTED |
|---|---|---|---|---|
| 22 | Bright Blue | Blk-W | Silver | Blk-DB-Sil |
| 27 | Steel Blue | Blk-W | Silver | Blk-DB-Sil |
| 42 | Bright Green | Blk-W | Silver | Blk-N-MS-Sil |
| 70 | Orange Flame | Blk-W | Silver | Blk-N-MS |
| 74 | Dark Red | Blk-W | Silver | Blk-N-DR-MS-Sil |
| 76 | Mille Miglia Red | Blk-W | Silver | Blk-N-DR-MS-Sil |
| 67 | Medium Saddle | Blk-W | Silver | Blk-N-MS |
| 13 | Silver | Blk-W | Silver | Blk-DB-DR-MS-Sil |
| 10 | Classic White | Blk-W | Silver | Blk-DB-N-DR-MS-Sil |
| 56 | Bright Yellow | Blk-W | Silver | Blk-N-MS |

Interior Codes: Blk/V=19V; Blk/L=192; DB/V=26V; DB/L=262; Sil/V=14V; Sil/L=142; N/V=601; MS/V=65V; MS/L=652; DR/V=73V; DR/L=732.

ABBREVIATIONS: Blk = Black, DB = Dark Blue, Sil = Silver, N = Neutral, MS = Medium Saddle, DR = Dark Red, W = White, L=Leather, V=Vinyl

• Black, Dark Blue, Red, Saddle and Silver were available in leather.
• Steel Blue was offered only for three months.

# 1976 CORVETTE

Production: 46,558

## 1976 SERIAL NUMBERS

Body and Chassis: 1Z37L6S400001 through 1Z37L6S446558
- 5th digit varies as follows: L = Base
  - X = L-82

Engine Suffix: CLM, CLR, CLS, CHC, CHR, CKC, CKW, CKX.

## 1976 FACTS

- The "Corvette" trim identification on the rear bumper of the 1976 model changed slightly from the previous year and the front bumper was redesigned again, but the external appearance of the 1976 was very close to the 1975.

- The vents on the rear deck (just behind the window) were removed from the 1976 model.

- Chevrolet promoted a new "sport" steering wheel for the 1976 model, but the wheel was in fact the same as used on the Vega. Complaints from outraged Corvette enthusiasts contributed to Chevrolet's decision to replace the wheel in the 1977 model.

- The 1976 model Corvette came factory equipped with GM's new "freedom" battery, a completely sealed, maintenance free unit.

- The 1976 model Corvette finally got the aluminum wheels first announced as available for the 1973 model. GM had initially contracted a California vendor to produce the wheels in 1973, but quality problems led to GM's refusal to accept and offer the wheels during that model year. In spite of efforts to recall all wheels of this first run, some are in the hands of collectors. The new wheel offered for the 1976 model was of the same design as the earlier offering, but was produced by Kelsey-Hayes in their Mexican facility (and is identified as such on the inside surface). When purchased on the 1976 model, the YJ8 Aluminum Wheel option includes only four wheels, with a standard steel spare. This was not the case with the aluminum wheels of the 1963 through 1967 period, but was done to hold the price in line for the YJ8 option.

- The 1976 Corvette received a partial steel underbelly in the forward section. This was done for added rigidity and to better isolate the passenger compartment from the temperatures being created by the engines which were calibrated to run hotter (and thus more efficiently) to offset some of the emissions-related power losses.

- The carburetor air induction system was revised in 1976 from the previous system of drawing air in at the rear of the hood, to an over-the-radiator source. The change was noise-reduction related, since the proximity of the rear-hood induction to the passenger compartment produced some quite audible howling sound irritation to driver and passengers.

- 1976 is the last year for a unique Corvette radio. The console was redesigned the following year to allow standard Delco radios to be used.

• Some items, such as the standard (mandatory option) leather interior, sunvisors, and interior lighting normally associated with the 1977 model actually appeared in late 1976.

# 1976 OPTIONS

| RPO # | DESCRIPTION | UNITS* | RETAIL $ |
|---|---|---|---|
| 1YZ37 | Base Corvette Sport Coupe | 46558 | 7604.85 |
| — | Custom Interior Trim | - | 164.00 |
| A31 | Power Windows | 38700 | 107.00 |
| C49 | Rear Window Defogger | 24960 | 78.00 |
| C60 | Air Conditioning | 40787 | 523.00 |
| FE7 | Gymkhana Suspension | 5368 | 35.00 |
| — | Positraction Axle, Optional Ratio | 1371 | 13.00 |
| J50 | Power Brakes | 46558 | 59.00 |
| L82 | Optional 210 HP, 350 CI Engine | 5720 | 481.00 |
| M21 | 4-Speed Close Ratio Transmission | 2088 | nc |
| M40 | Turbo Hydramatic Transmission | 36625 | nc |
| N37 | Tilt-Telescopic Steering Column | 41797 | 95.00 |
| N40 | Power Steering | 46385 | 151.00 |
| QRM | White Stripe SBR Tires, GR70x15 | 3992 | 37.00 |
| QRZ | White Letter SBR Tires, GR70x15 | 39923 | 51.00 |
| U58 | AM-FM Stereo Radio | 34272 | 281.00 |
| U69 | AM-FM Radio | 11083 | 187.00 |
| UA1 | Heavy Duty Battery | 25909 | 16.00 |
| UF1 | Map Light | 35361 | 10.00 |
| YJ8 | Aluminum Wheels | 6253 | 299.00 |

*Sales during production year according to Chevrolet records.

• The cost of the M40 Automatic Transmission with the L-82 engine option was $134.00.

• The rear window defogger in 1976 was of the heated glass element type.

• Base price includes standard 350 CI, 180 HP engine.

• Option list does not include additional items available as dealer installed accessories.

# 1976 COLORS

| CODE | EXTERIOR | SOFT TOP | WHEELS | INTERIORS GM SUGGESTED |
|---|---|---|---|---|
| 22 | Bright Blue | n/a | Silver | Blk-SG |
| 69 | Dark Brown | n/a | Silver | Blk-Buc-DB-W |
| 64 | Buckskin | n/a | Silver | Blk-F-Buc-DB-W |
| 33 | Dark Green | n/a | Silver | Blk-Buc-SG-BG-W |
| 37 | Mahogany | n/a | Silver | Blk-F-Buc-SG-W |
| 70 | Orange Flame | n/a | Silver | Blk-Buc-DB |
| 72 | Red | n/a | Silver | Blk-F-Buc-SG-W |
| 13 | Silver | n/a | Silver | Blk-F-Buc-SG-BG-W |
| 10 | Classic White | n/a | Silver | Blk-F-Buc-SG-DB-BG-W |
| 56 | Bright Yellow | n/a | Silver | Blk-DB |

Interior Codes: Blk/V=19V; Blk/L=192; F/V=71V; F/L=712; Buc/V=64V; Buc/L=642; SG/L=152; BG/L=322; DB/L=692; W/V=15V; W/L=152.

ABBREVIATIONS: Blk = Black, F = Firethorn, Buc = Buckskin, SG = Smoked Grey, DB = Dark Brown!, BG = Blue-Green, W = White, L=Leather, V=Vinyl

# 1977 CORVETTE

Production: 49,213

## 1977 SERIAL NUMBERS

Body and Chassis: 1Z37L7S400001 through 1Z37L7S449213
- 5th digit varies as follows: L = Base
X = L82

Engine Suffix: CKZ, CLA, CLB, CLC, CLD, CLF, CKD, CHD

## 1977 FACTS

- The interior of the 1977 model was the most restyled since the introduction of the new body style in 1968. A completely new console houses new heater and air conditioning controls. The new console was designed to allow more radio depth so that standard GM radios could be used. Previously, the Corvette radio was unique and the Corvette's production volume would not justify development of stereo tape and CB units. But starting with the 1977 model, more options became available since standard GM line Delco radios could be used.

- A new steering column in 1977 permitted designers to move the steering wheel of the 1977 Corvette two inches closer to the dash. In addition to creating a more ''arms out'' driving position, the change makes entry and exit easier. The steering wheel and horn button were also redesigned.

- The luggage rack of the 1977 models was redesigned to hold the top roof panels. This permitted the luggage compartment to be used while the roof panels were off the car, something that was extremely restricted in prior years.

- The CC1 glass roof panels, listed as options in early 1977, were not available during the 1977 model year. The agreement between GM and the supplying vendor was cancelled, reportedly after dispute regarding the exclusive marketing of the panels by GM. GM introduced its own glass panels in mid-1978, again with the CC1 order designation. The manufacturer of the panels that were to be available in 1977 marketed them under the trade name ''moon roofs'' and they became a quite popular aftermarket item.

- Early in 1977 production , the burglar alarm switch was moved from the left fender to the driver's door lock.

- Leather seats are standard equipment in 1977 Corvettes and, for the first time, cloth seats trimmed in leather could be ordered.

- The headlight dimmer switch, windshield wiper and windshield washer controls are all located on steering column stalks in 1977 models.

- 1977 is the first year of availability of Cruise Control on Corvettes (Automatic transmission only).

- The sunshades in the 1977 model Corvette were redesigned to permit swinging to the side to block door window sun entry.

- Early 1977 models had no fender cross flags.

- The manual transmission shift lever was made an inch longer to permit easier handbrake operation.

• The interior rearview mirror in the 1977 model was moved to the windshield from a previous mounting just above the windshield, minimizing vibration.

## 1977 OPTIONS

| RPO # | DESCRIPTION | UNITS* | RETAIL $ |
|---|---|---|---|
| 1YZ37 | Base Corvette Sport Coupe | 49213 | 8647.65 |
| A31 | Power Windows | 44341 | 116.00 |
| B32 | Color Keyed Floor Mats | 36763 | 22.00 |
| C49 | Rear Window Defogger | 30411 | 84.00 |
| C60 | Air Conditioning | 45249 | 553.00 |
| D35 | Sport Mirrors | 20206 | 36.00 |
| FE7 | Gymkhana Suspension | 7269 | 38.00 |
| G95 | Positraction Axle, Optional Ratio | 972 | 14.00 |
| K30 | Cruise Control | 29161 | 88.00 |
| L82 | Optional 210 HP, 350 CI Engine | 6148 | 495.00 |
| M21 | 4-Speed Close Ratio Transmission | 2060 | nc |
| M40 | Turbo Hydramatic Automatic Transmission | 41231 | nc |
| N37 | Tilt-Telescopic Steering Column | 46487 | 165.00 |
| QRZ | White Letter SBR Tires, GR70x15 | 46227 | 57.00 |
| UA1 | Heavy Duty Battery | 32882 | 17.00 |
| U58 | AM-FM Stereo Radio | 18483 | 281.00 |
| U69 | AM-FM Radio | 4700 | 187.00 |
| UM2 | AM-FM Stereo Radio W/Tape System | 24603 | 414.00 |
| V54 | Luggage And Roof Panel Rack | - | 73.00 |
| YJ8 | Aluminum Wheels | 12646 | 321.00 |
| ZN1 | Trailer Package | 289 | 83.00 |
| ZX2 | Convenience Group | 40872 | 22.00 |

*Sales during production year according to Chevrolet records.

• The cost of the M40 Automatic Transmission with the L-82 engine option was $146.00.

• Power steering, power brakes and leather (deluxe) interior were all made standard equipment in 1977. They were mandatory options late in 1976.

• Base price includes standard 350 CI, 180 HP engine.

## 1977 COLORS

| CODE | EXTERIOR | SOFT TOP | WHEELS | INTERIORS GM SUGGESTED |
|---|---|---|---|---|
| 19 | Black | n/a | Silver | Blk-Buc-R-SG-W |
| 28 | Corvette Dark Blue | n/a | Silver | Blk-Blu-Buc-SG-W |
| 26 | Corvette Light Blue | n/a | Silver | Blk-SG-W |
| 66 | Corvette Orange | n/a | Silver | Blk-Br-Buc |
| 83 | Corvette Dark Red | n/a | Silver | Blk-Buc-SG |
| 72 | Medium Red | n/a | Silver | Blk-Buc-R-SG-W |
| 13 | Silver | n/a | Silver | Blk-Blu-R-SG-W |
| 80 | Corvette Tan | n/a | Silver | Blk-Br-Buc-R-W |
| 10 | Classic White | n/a | Silver | Blk-Blu-Br-Buc-R-SG-W |
| 52 | Corvette Yellow | n/a | Silver | Blk-Br |

**Interior Codes:** Blk/C=19C; Blk/L=192; Buc/C=64C; Buc/L=642; R/C=72C; R/L=722; SG/C=15C; SG/L=152; Blu/C=27C; Blu/L=272; Br/C=69C; Br/L=692.

ABBREVIATIONS: Blk = Black, Buc = Buckskin, R = Red, SG = Smoked Grey, W = White, Blu = Blue, Br = Brown, L=Leather, C=Cloth

• All interiors genuine leather or leather/cloth combination.

# 1978 CORVETTE

Production: 40,274 std, 6,502 pace replica

## 1978 SERIAL NUMBERS

Body and Chassis: 1Z87L8S400001 through 1Z87L8S440274
1Z87L8S900001 through 1Z87L8S906502 (Pace Car)

- 5th digit varies as follows: L = Base    4 = L82

Engine Suffix:  CLR: L48 Calif        CLM: L48 Auto
CLS: L48 Hi Alt       CMR: L82 4-Speed
CUT: L48 Auto-w/fed   CMS: L-82 Auto
CHW: L48 4-Speed

## 1978 FACTS

• Chevrolet celebrated the silver anniversary of the Corvette by introducing the most restyled Corvette since the 1968 model. Most apparent change was the rear end which was given a large window in true "fastback" style. The change created significantly more luggage space behind the seats. A retracting cover was also added to the rear storage space to hide the contents from peering eyes or damaging sun.

• The interior of the 1978 model was also redesigned. The driver instruments (speedometer and tachometer) were redone in a squarish, more vertical mode. A glove box was added. Inner door panels were completely new, featuring removable arm rests rather than the molded-in style common to Corvettes since 1965. Windshield wiper and washer controls were moved back to the dash, though the light dimmer switch remained on the steering column.

• New "25th Anniversary" emblems are used on the exterior and interior.

• The fuel tank in the 1978 model was redesigned to hold 24 gallons, rather than the 17+ of previous years.

• The theft alarm system was modified in the 1978 model Corvettes to include monitoring of the roof panels.

• The 1978 Corvette was chosen as the pace car for the Indianapolis 500 race. To commemorate the event, Chevrolet introduced a "limited edition" Pace Car Corvette. The design features and build quantities of this car led to considerable confusion. Initially, the Pace Car was to have been two-tone silver with red striping. It was to have special Goodyear tires with "Corvette" sidewalls and the build quantity was reported to be 1000 cars. After several changes, the final paint scheme became black over a silver bottom with red striping. The Goodyear "Corvette" tires were dropped as unfeasible and the build quantity became one for each Chevrolet dealer (approximately 6000) plus extras. The final count was 6502.

• Wider "60" series tires became available on the 1978 Corvette and required fender trimming by the factory for clearance. Standard size remained "70" series radials.

• The "Silver Anniversary" paint option consists of two-tone silver (light silver top surface and darker silver bottom with silver dividing tape stripes). Sport mirrors and aluminum wheels were mandatory options.

# 1978 OPTIONS

| RPO # | DESCRIPTION | UNITS* | RETAIL $ |
|---|---|---|---|
| 1YZ87 | Corvette Sport Coupe | 40274 | 9351.89 |
| 1YZ87/78 | Limited Edition Corvette (Pace Car) | 6502 | 13653.21 |
| A31 | Power Windows | 36931 | 130.00 |
| AU3 | Power Door Locks | 12187 | 120.00 |
| B2Z | Silver Anniversary Paint | 15283 | 399.00 |
| CC1 | Removable Glass Roof Panels | 972 | 349.00 |
| C49 | Rear Window Defogger | 30912 | 95.00 |
| C60 | Air Conditioning | 37638 | 605.00 |
| D35 | Sport Mirrors | 38405 | 40.00 |
| FE7 | Gymkhana Suspension | 12590 | 41.00 |
| G95 | Positraction Axle, Optional Highway Ratio | 382 | 15.00 |
| K30 | Cruise Control | 31608 | 99.00 |
| L82 | Optional 220 HP, 350 CI Engine | 12739 | 525.00 |
| M21 | 4-Speed Close Ratio Transmission | 3385 | nc |
| MX1 | Turbo Hydramatic Automatic Transmission | 38614 | nc |
| N37 | Tilt-Telescopic Steering Column | 37858 | 175.00 |
| QBS | White Letter SBR Tires, P255/60 R-15 | 18296 | 216.32 |
| QGR | White Letter SBR Tires, P225/70 R-15 | 26203 | 51.00 |
| UA1 | Heavy Duty Battery | 28243 | 18.00 |
| UM2 | AM-FM Stereo Radio W/Tape System | 20899 | 419.00 |
| UP6 | AM-FM Stereo Radio W/CB System | 7138 | 638.00 |
| U58 | AM-FM Stereo Radio | 10189 | 286.00 |
| U69 | AM-FM Radio | 2057 | 199.00 |
| U75 | Power Antenna | 23069 | 49.00 |
| U81 | Dual Rear Speakers | 12340 | 49.00 |
| YJ8 | Aluminum Wheels | 28008 | 340.00 |
| ZN1 | Trailer Package | 972 | 89.00 |
| ZX2 | Convenience Group | 37222 | 84.00 |

*Sales during production year according to Chevrolet records.

• The base price of the Pace Car includes options A31, AU3, CC1, C49, C60, D35, N37, QBS, UA1, UM2, U75, U81, YJ8 (with red accent) and ZX2. Added cost options are ZN1, YF5 (California Emissions), and K30. The UP6 radio could be substituted for UM2 at a cost of $170.00. Customer had choice of transmission, engine and cloth/leather interior.

# 1978 COLORS

| CODE | EXTERIOR | SOFT TOP | WHEELS | INTERIORS GM SUGGESTED |
|---|---|---|---|---|
| 59 | Corvette Light Beige | n/a | Silver | Blk-LB-DB-M |
| 19 | Black | n/a | Silver | Blk-LB-R-M-O |
| 83 | Corvette Dark Blue | n/a | Silver | DB-LB-O |
| 26 | Corvette Light Blue | n/a | Silver | DB |
| 89 | Corvette Dark Brown | n/a | Silver | DB-LB-O |
| 82 | Corvette Mahogany | n/a | Silver | Blk-LB-M-O |
| 72 | Corvette Red | n/a | Silver | Blk-LB-R-O |
| 13 | Silver | n/a | Silver | Blk-DB-R-M |
| 13 | Silver Anniversary | n/a | Silver | Blk-R -O |
| 10 | Classic White | n/a | Silver | Blk-DB-LB-R-M-O |
| 52 | Corvette Yellow | n/a | Silver | Blk-O |

Interior Codes: Blk/C=19C; Blk/L=192; LB/C=59C; LB/L=592; DB/C=29C; DB/L=292; M/C=76C; M/L=762; R/C=72C; R/L=722; O/C=12C; O/L=122; Silver/C/Pace=15C; Silver/L/Pace=152.

ABBREVIATIONS: Blk = Black, LB = Light Beige, DB = Dark Blue, M = Mahogany, R = Red, O = Oyster, L=Leather, C=Cloth

# 1979 CORVETTE

Production: 53,807

## 1979 SERIAL NUMBERS

Body and Chassis: 1Z8789S400001 through 1Z8789S453807

- 5th digit varies as follows: 8=L-48
  4=L-82

Engine Suffix: ZAA: L-48 4-Speed     ZAD: L-48 Hi Alt
         ZAB: L-48 Auto/Fed     ZBA: L-82 4-Speed
         ZAC: L-48 Calif            ZBB: L-82 Auto

## 1979 FACTS

- The "anniversary" emblems used for one model year (1978) were deleted and replaced with the elongated-style Corvette crossed flag emblems.

- The "high back" bucket seats introduced in 1978 on the limited edition pace car were made standard equipment in the 1979 model. These seats feature extensive use of plastics in the frame structure for weight reduction of about 12 pounds per seat. The new seat design has better side bolster support and the backs break forward at a central location to permit easier access to the rear storage compartment. Inertia locking mechanisms restrain the back rest upon sudden deceleration, eliminating the need for manually operated locks. Both passenger and driver seat tracks were redesigned in 1979 to permit an additional inch of forward travel. The seats could be ordered in various color combinations of leather and cloth-leather.

- The fuel filler of 1979 models was redesigned to make leaded fuel conversions more difficult.

- In 1978, Corvettes equipped with manual transmissions were equipped with stiffer shock absorbers regardless of customer preference. In 1979, this practice was stopped and the standard softer suspension came with all base Corvettes regardless of transmission choice.

- Modifications to the exhaust systems of 1979 models, including a new "open flow" muffler design, to reduce back-pressure resulted in an addition of approximately five horsepower to both the base L-48 and optional L-82 engines. Additionally, the L-48 picked up about another five horsepower with a low-restriction, dual-snorkle air intake, previously used on just L-82 models.

- The standard rear axle ratio of 1979 models equipped with automatic transmissions changed from 3.08:1 to 3.55:1.

- In 1979, an AM-FM radio became standard equipment.

- In 1979, an illuminated visor-mirror combination became available for the first time (passenger side only).

- Tungsten-Halogen headlight beams were phased into 1979 production early in the model year for increased visibility. These replaced only the high-beam units.

- The mirrored-tint glass roof panels, introduced on the Pace Car, became optional on late 1978 models and all 1979 models.

• Bolt-on front and rear spoilers, ala pace car, became optional in 1979 as a package. Wind tunnel tests of pace car Corvettes proved the spoiler package capable of decreasing drag by about 15%, which translates to a fuel-economy increase of nearly one-half mile-per-gallon.

# 1979 OPTIONS

| RPO # | DESCRIPTION | UNITS* | RETAIL $ |
|---|---|---|---|
| 1YZ87 | Corvette Sport Coupe | 53807 | 10220.23 |
| A31 | Power Windows | 20631 | 141.00 |
| AU3 | Power Door Locks | 9054 | 131.00 |
| CC1 | Removable Glass Roof Panels | 14480 | 365.00 |
| C49 | Rear Window Defogger | 41587 | 102.00 |
| C60 | Air Conditioning | 47136 | 635.00 |
| D35 | Sport Mirrors | 48211 | 45.00 |
| D80 | Spoilers | 6853 | 265.00 |
| FE7 | Gymkhana Suspension | 12321 | 49.00 |
| F51 | Heavy Duty Shock Absorbers | 2164 | 33.00 |
| G95 | Highway ratio rear axle | 428 | 19.00 |
| K30 | Cruise Control | 34445 | 113.00 |
| L82 | Optional 225 HP, 350 CI Engine | 14516 | 565.00 |
| MM4 | 4-Speed Transmission, Close Ratio | 4062 | nc |
| MX1 | Turbo-Hydramatic Automatic Transmission | 41454 | nc |
| N37 | Tilt-telescopic Steering Column | 47463 | 190.00 |
| N90 | Aluminum Wheels | 33741 | 380.00 |
| QGR | White Letter SBR Tires, P225/70 R-15 | 29603 | 54.00 |
| QBS | White Letter Aramid Tires, P255/60 R-15 | 17920 | 226.20 |
| U58 | AM/FM Stereo Radio | 9256 | 90.00 |
| UM2 | AM/FM Stereo Radio w/tape | 21435 | 228.00 |
| UN3 | AM/FM Stereo Radio w/cassette | 12110 | 234.00 |
| UP6 | AM/FM Stereo Radio w/CB/power antenna | 4483 | 439.00 |
| U75 | Power Antenna | 35730 | 52.00 |
| U81 | Dual Rear Speakers | 37754 | 52.00 |
| UA1 | Heavy Duty Battery | 3405 | 21.00 |
| ZN1 | Trailer Package | 1001 | 98.00 |
| ZQ2 | Power Windows and Door Locks | 28465 | 272.00 |
| ZX2 | Convenience Group | 41530 | 94.00 |

*Sales during production year according to Chevrolet records.

# 1979 COLORS

| CODE | EXTERIOR | SOFT TOP | WHEELS | INTERIORS GM SUGGESTED |
|---|---|---|---|---|
| 59 | Corvette Light Beige | n/a | Silver | Blk, DBR, LB, DG |
| 19 | Black | n/a | Silver | Blk, LB, O |
| 83 | Corvette Dark Blue | n/a | Silver | DB, LB, O |
| 28 | Corvette Light Blue | n/a | Silver | DB |
| 82 | Corvette Dark Brown | n/a | Silver | DBR, LB |
| 58 | Corvette Dark Green | n/a | Silver | LB, DG, O |
| 72 | Corvette Red | n/a | Silver | Blk, LB, R, O |
| 13 | Silver | n/a | Silver* | Blk, DB, R, DG |
| 52 | Corvette Yellow | n/a | Silver | Blk, O |
| 10 | Classic White | n/a | Silver | Blk, DB, DBR, LB, R, DG, O |

Interior Codes: Blk/L=192; LB/C=59C; LB/L=592; DB/C=29C; DB/L=292; R/L=722; O/C=12C; O/L=122; DG/C=49C; DG/L=492.

ABBREVIATIONS: Blk=Black, DB=Dark Blue, DBR=Dark Brown, LB=Light Beige, R=Red, DG=Dark Green, O=Oyster, C=Cloth, L=Leather

# 1980 CORVETTE

Production: 40,614

## 1980 SERIAL NUMBERS

Body and Chassis: 1Z878AS400001 through 1Z878AS440614
- 5th digit varies as follows: 8=L-48, 6=L-82, H=LG4

Engine Suffix: ZCA: LG4 (305) Calif
ZAM: L-48 (350) 4-Speed
ZAK: L-48 (350) Auto

ZBD: L-82 (350) 4-Speed
ZBC: L-82 (350) Auto

## 1980 FACTS

- The 1980 models featured completely new front and rear bumper "caps" with integral spoilers for each. The redesigned front end added a nearly 50% increase in radiator air flow. The total spoiler package achieves a drag coefficient reduction from .503 to .443, compared to previous models without add-on spoilers.

- The top speedometer reading for 1980 Corvettes was reduced to 85 mph by federal mandate.

- The crossed flag Corvette emblem was redesigned again for 1980; the new design is similar to previous emblems, but more elongated in shape.

- Tilt-telescopic steering became standard equipment.

- The three storage compartments behind the seats were reduced to two in the 1980 model. The battery remained in its own compartment behind the driver, but the center and passenger-side compartments were combined with one access door.

- The 1980 model should go down in Corvette history as the first year of significant weight reductions. Engineers trimmed weight from several locations including lower density roof panels, reduced gage in hood and outer doors, thinner door and windshield glass, frame gage reduction, and a new aluminum differential housing and cross member. The differential and crossmember project alone saved 40 pounds.

- The aluminum intake manifold previously standard on the L-82 engines became standard on the L-48 in 1980 as well.

- For the first time since 1974, two different displacement engines were available in Corvettes, though not exactly optional. Because of tightened emission standards in California, Chevrolet chose not to certify its 350 CI engines there, so California buyers of 1980 Corvettes had to accept a 305 CI engine. This engine was the only one available to California buyers and it was not available anywhere else.

- The California 305 engine was fitted with innovative stainless steel tubular exhaust headers with an oxygen sensor in a "closed loop" system. Despite its displacement and emission restrictions, the 305 engine was rated at 180 HP, just 10 less than the base L-48 of other states.

- Though two rear axles are fitted to 1980 Corvettes depending on 4-speed or automatic transmission, both have ratios of 3.07:1 for economy. There were no optional ratios.

- The fake bumperettes common to the front and rear flexible bumpers of several previous model Corvettes were deleted from the 1980 models.
- Air conditioning was standard equipment in 1980.
- The power door lock button moved from the lower part of the door panel to the upper corner.

## 1980 OPTIONS

| RPO # | DESCRIPTION | UNITS* | RETAIL $ |
|-------|-------------|--------|----------|
| 1YZ87 | Corvette Sport Coupe | 40614 | 13140.24 |
| AU3 | Power Door Locks | 32692 | 140.00 |
| CC1 | Removable Glass Roof Panels | 19695 | 391.00 |
| C49 | Rear Window Defogger | 36589 | 109.00 |
| FE7 | Gymkhana Suspension | 9907 | 55.00 |
| F51 | Heavy Duty Shock Absorbers | 1695 | 35.00 |
| K30 | Cruise Control | 30821 | 123.00 |
| LG4 | 180 HP, 305 CI Engine (Req'd California) | 3221 | (50.00) |
| L82 | 230 HP, 350 CI Engine | 5069 | 595.00 |
| MM4 | 4-Speed Transmission | 5726 | nc |
| MX1 | Turbo-Hydramatic Automatic Transmission | 34838 | nc |
| N90 | Aluminum Wheels | 34128 | 407.00 |
| QGB | White Letter SBR Tires, P225/70 R-15 | 26208 | 62.00 |
| QXH | White Letter SBR Tires, P255/60 R-15 | 13140 | 426.16 |
| UA1 | Heavy Duty Battery | 1337 | 22.00 |
| U58 | AM/FM Stereo Radio | 6136 | 46.00 |
| UM2 | AM/FM Stereo Radio w/8-track tape | 15708 | 155.00 |
| UN3 | AM/FM Stereo Radio w/cassette tape | 15148 | 168.00 |
| UP6 | AM/FM Stereo Radio w/CB / power antenna | 2434 | 391.00 |
| U75 | Power Antenna | 32863 | 56.00 |
| UL5 | Radio Delete | 201 | (126.00) |
| U81 | Dual Rear Speakers | 36650 | 52.00 |
| V54 | Roof Panel Carrier | 3755 | 125.00 |
| YF5 | California Emissions | 3221 | 250.00 |
| ZN1 | Trailer Package | 796 | 105.00 |

*Sales during production year according to Chevrolet records.

- The L48 base engine in 1980 was 190 horsepower.

## 1980 COLORS

| CODE | EXTERIOR | SOFT TOP | WHEELS | INTERIORS GM SUGGESTED |
|------|----------|----------|--------|------------------------|
| 19 | Black | n/a | Silver | Blk, O, R, DS |
| 13 | Silver | n/a | Silver | Blk, R, DB, CL |
| 58 | Dark Green | n/a | Silver | O, DS |
| 83 | Red | n/a | Silver | Blk, O, R, DS |
| 52 | Yellow | n/a | Silver | Blk, O |
| 28 | Dark Blue | n/a | Silver | O, DB, DS |
| 59 | Frost Beige | n/a | Silver | Blk, DB, CL, DS |
| 76 | Dark Claret | n/a | Silver | O, CL, DS |
| 47 | Dark Brown | n/a | Silver | DS |
| 10 | White | n/a | Silver | Blk, O, R, DB, CL, DS |

Interior Codes: Blk/L=192; O/C=12C; O/L=122; R/L=722; DB/C=29C; DB/L=292; CL/C=79C; CL/L=792; DS/C=59C; DS/L=592.

ABBREVIATIONS: Blk=Black, O=Oyster, R=Red, DB=Dark Blue, CL=Claret, DS=Doeskin, C=Cloth, L=Leather

# 1981 CORVETTE

## 1981 SERIAL NUMBERS

**Body and Chassis:** 1G1AY8764BS400001 thru 1G1AY8764BS431611
(St. Louis)
1G1AY8764B5100001 thru 1G1AY8764B5108995
(Bowling Green)
- Ninth digit is a check code and varies

**Engine Suffix:** ZDA: 4-Speed      ZDB: Auto/Calif
ZDD: Auto           ZDC: 4-speed/Calif

## 1981 FACTS

- Exterior styling of the 1981 model was carried over from 1980. Emblems did change slightly.

- The 350 CI engine was certified for use in California in 1981, so the Corvette returned to a standard displacement for all fifty states. There were no optional engines.

- The tubular stainless steel exhaust manifolds, used for 1980 California Corvettes with the 305 CI engine, were standard on all 1981 Corvettes.

- Chevrolet introduced a fiberglass reinforced monoleaf rear spring for 1981 Corvettes equipped with automatic transmissions and standard suspensions. The plastic spring weighed eight pounds compared to forty-four pounds for the steel unit replaced.

- Chevrolet's Computer Command Control system which was used on 1980 California Corvettes became standard equipment on all 1981 Corvettes. The system automatically adjusted ignition timing and carburetor air/fuel mixture.

- An improvement to the anti-theft alarm system was made in 1981 by the addition of an ignition interrupt, preventing engine starting.

- Engine cooling was improved in 1981, and the engine fan was reduced in size (to increase engine power) by the addition of an auxiliary electric cooling fan behind the radiator.

- New power assists for 1981 included a six-way electric seat (driver side only) and electrically adjusted remote control outside sport mirrors.

- The 1981 Corvette was the only model year to be built simultaneously in two locations. The first Corvette rolled off the new Bowling Green, Kentucky, assembly line on June 1, 1981. The last Corvette to be built at St. Louis was completed on August 1, 1981.

- Construction of Corvettes in two facilities during 1981 created some confusion regarding paint and colors. St. Louis continued to use lacquer right up to the last Corvette built there, but a new process was developed for Bowling Green Corvettes which used enamel basecoats followed by clear topcoats. It is thought by some that all solid color 1981 models were built in St. Louis and all two-tones in Bowling Green. In fact, both styles were built at both plants, though the number of two-tones built in St. Louis was small. The paints used by the two facilities were different and incompatible.

• The 1981 Corvette was the last to have a four-speed transmission available until the introduction of a completely new four-speed with electric overdrive after the start of 1984 production.

# 1981 OPTIONS

| RPO # | DESCRIPTION | UNITS* | RETAIL $ |
|-------|-------------|--------|----------|
| 1YY87 | Corvette Sport Coupe | 40606 | 16258.52 |
| AU3 | Power Door Locks | 36322 | 145.00 |
| A42 | Power Driver Seat | 29200 | 183.00 |
| CC1 | Removable Glass Roof Panels | 29095 | 414.00 |
| C49 | Rear Window Defogger | 36893 | 119.00 |
| DG7 | Electric Sport Mirrors | 13567 | 117.00 |
| D84 | Two-Tone Exterior Paint | 5352 | 399.00 |
| FE7 | Gymkhana Suspension | 7803 | 57.00 |
| F51 | Heavy Duty Shock Absorbers | 1128 | 37.00 |
| G92 | Performance Rear Axle | 2400 | 20.00 |
| K35 | Cruise Control | 32522 | 155.00 |
| L81 | 190 HP, 350 CI Engine (standard) | 40606 | nc |
| MM4 | 4-Speed Transmission | 5757 | nc |
| N90 | Aluminum Wheels | 36485 | 428.00 |
| QGR | White Letter SBR Tires, P225/70R-15 | 21939 | 72.00 |
| QXH | White Letter SBR Tires, P255/60R-15 | 18004 | 491.92 |
| UL5 | Radio Delete | 315 | (118.00) |
| UM4 | Elect Tuned AM/FM Stereo w/8-track | 8262 | 386.00 |
| UM5 | Elect Tuned AM/FM Stereo w/8-track/CB | 792 | 712.00 |
| UM6 | Elect Tuned AM/FM Stereo w/cassette | 22892 | 423.00 |
| UN5 | Elect Tuned AM/FM Stereo w/cassette/CB | 2349 | 750.00 |
| U58 | AM/FM Stereo Radio | 5145 | 95.00 |
| U75 | Power Antenna | 32903 | 55.00 |
| V54 | Roof Panel Carrier | 3303 | 135.00 |
| YF5 | California Emissions | 4951 | 46.00 |
| ZN1 | Trailer Package | 916 | 110.00 |

*Sales during production year according to Chevrolet records.

# 1981 COLORS

| CODE | EXTERIOR | SOFT TOP | WHEELS | INTERIORS GM SUGGESTED |
|------|----------|----------|--------|------------------------|
| 75 | Red | n/a | Silver | CM, CH, DR, SGY |
| 52 | Yellow | n/a | Silver | CH |
| 19 | Black | n/a | Silver | CM, CH, MR, SGY |
| 10 | White | n/a | Silver | CM, CH, DR, MR, DB, SGY |
| 59 | Beige | n/a | Silver | CM, CH |
| 13 | Silver Metallic | n/a | Silver | CM, CH, DR, MR, SGY |
| 28 | Dark Blue Metallic | n/a | Silver | CM, DB, SGY |
| 24 | Bright Blue Metallic | n/a | Silver | CM, DB, CH, SGY |
| 79 | Maroon Metallic | n/a | Silver | CM, DR, SGY |
| 84 | Charcoal Metallic | n/a | Silver | CH, DR, MR, SGY |
| 33/38M | Silver/Dark Blue* | n/a | Silver | DB, SGY |
| 50/74M | Beige/Dark Bronze* | n/a | Silver | CM |
| 33/39M | Silver/Charcoal* | n/a | Silver | CH, SGY |
| 89/98M | Claret/Dark Claret* | n/a | Silver | DR, SGY |

*Bowling Green colors.

Interior Codes: CM/L = 642; CM/C = 64C; CH/L = 192; CH/C = 19C; DR/L = 672; DR/C = 67C; MR/L = 752; DB/L = 292; DB/C = 29C; SGY/L = 152.

ABBREVIATIONS: CM = Camel, CH = Charcoal, DR = Dark Red, MR = Medium Red, DB = Dark Blue, SGY = Silver Gray, C = Cloth, L = Leather.

# 1982 CORVETTE

Production: 18,648 std, 6,759 collector

## 1982 SERIAL NUMBERS

Body and Chassis: 1G1AY8786C5100001 thru 1G1AY8786C5125407
- Sixth digit is a zero for the Collector Edition
- Ninth digit is a check code and varies

Engine Suffix: ZBA: Automatic
ZBC: Automatic/California

## 1982 FACTS

- The 1982 Corvette was the last of a generation of Corvettes. Its basic body shape dated to 1968, and its chassis to 1963.

- A manual transmission was not available in the 1982 Corvette.

- Hoods of 1982 models had solenoid operated doors to direct fresh air directly into the air cleaner during full throttle.

- The transmission in the 1982 Corvette was a new four-speed automatic unit with a torque converter clutch which operated in the top three gears.

- Chevrolet introduced "cross fire injection" on the 1982 model. This was not fuel injection of the type available in 1957-1965 Corvettes. Rather, it combined two "injectors" with Chevrolet's Computer Command Control system to achieve better economy, driveability, and performance through more precise metering of the fuel. The Computer Command Control itself was refined in 1982 such that it was capable of making eighty adjustments per second compared to ten the previous year.

- The new fuel metering system of the 1982 model included a positive fuel shutoff to prevent engine "dieseling."

- The charcoal air filtering element of the 1981 model was replaced with a paper element in the cross fire injection 1982.

- The new automatic transmission used a higher first gear ratio (3.07:1) for improved acceleration.

- To honor the 1982 model's status as the last of a breed, Chevrolet offered a "Collector's Edition." The Collector Corvette differed from the standard 1982 in several ways. In addition to a higher level of standard features optional on standard models, the Collector Edition had a lifting rear glass, special wheels styled after the optional "bolt-on" 1967 aluminum wheels, unique gold/silver exterior paint and a matching gold/silver interior. There were also a number of exquisite detail changes such as cloisonne emblems.

- The exhaust system of the 1982 was redesigned with a smaller and lighter catalytic converter. Also, the exhaust pipes leading into the converter were redesigned to deliver hotter exhaust gases to the converter to increase its efficiency.

- 1982 exterior styling was a carry-over from the previous year, but there were detail differences. Easiest identification is by the "cross fire injection" side fender emblems which all 1982 models have.

- 1982 was the first complete model year to be built in the new plant in Bowling Green, Kentucky. Production actually started in the 1981 model year.

- The 1982 Collector Edition Corvette was the first in history to crack the $20,000 base sticker barrier. Its base was $22,537.59.
- The Collector Edition carried a special serial number.

## 1982 OPTIONS

| RPO # | DESCRIPTION | UNITS* | RETAIL $ |
|---|---|---|---|
| 1YY87 | Corvette Sport Coupe | 18648 | 18290.07 |
| 1YY07 | Collector Edition Hatchback | 6759 | 22537.59 |
| AG9 | Power Driver Seat | 22585 | 197.00 |
| AU3 | Power Door Locks | 23936 | 155.00 |
| CC1 | Removable Glass Roof Panels | 14763 | 443.00 |
| C49 | Rear Window Defogger | 16886 | 129.00 |
| DG7 | Electric Sport Mirrors | 20301 | 125.00 |
| D84 | Two-Tone Exterior Paint | 4871 | 428.00 |
| FE7 | Gymkhana Suspension | 5457 | 61.00 |
| K35 | Cruise Control | 24313 | 165.00 |
| L83 | 200 HP, 350 TBI Engine (std) | 25407 | nc |
| N90 | Aluminum Wheels | 16844 | 458.00 |
| QGR | White Letter SBR Tires, P225/70R-15 | 5932 | 80.00 |
| QXH | White Letter SBR Tires, P255/60R-15 | 19070 | 542.52 |
| UL5 | Radio Delete | 150 | (124.00) |
| UM4 | Elect Tuned AM/FM Stereo 8-track | 923 | 386.00 |
| UM6 | Elect Tuned AM/FM Stereo cassette | 20355 | 423.00 |
| UN5 | Elect Tuned AM/FM Stereo cassette/CB | 1987 | **755.00 |
| U58 | AM/FM Stereo Radio | 1533 | 101.00 |
| U75 | Power Antenna | 15557 | 60.00 |
| VO8 | Heavy Duty Cooling | 6006 | 57.00 |
| V54 | Roof Panel Carrier | 1992 | 144.00 |
| YF5 | California Emissions | 2725 | nc |

*Sales during production year according to Chevrolet records.
**$695 if purchased with Collector Edition.

## 1982 COLORS

| CODE | EXTERIOR | SOFT TOP | WHEELS | INTERIORS GM SUGGESTED |
|---|---|---|---|---|
| 19 | Black | n/a | Silver | CM, CH, DR, SGY, SGN |
| 31 | Bright Blue | n/a | Silver | CM, CH, DB, SGY |
| 26 | Dark Blue | n/a | Silver | CM, DB, SGY |
| 24 | Silver Blue | n/a | Silver | CM, CH, SGY |
| 39 | Charcoal | n/a | Silver | CH, DR, SGY |
| 99 | Dark Claret | n/a | Silver | CM, DR, SGY |
| 56 | Gold | n/a | Silver | CM, CH |
| 40 | Silver Green | n/a | Silver | CH, SGN |
| 70 | Red | n/a | Silver | CM, CH, DR, SGY |
| 13 | Silver | n/a | Silver | CH, DB, DR, SGY |
| 59 | Silver Beige | n/a | Silver | SB |
| 10 | White | n/a | Silver | CM, CH, DR, DB, SGY, SGN |
| 24/26M | Silver Blue/Dark Blue | n/a | Silver | DB, SGY |
| 13/99M | Silver/Dark Claret | n/a | Silver | DR, SGY |
| 13/39M | Silver/Charcoal | n/a | Silver | CH, DR, SGY |
| 10/13M | White/Silver | n/a | Silver | CH, SGY |

**Interior Codes:** CM/L = 642; CM/C = 64C; CH/L = 182; DR/L = 742; DR/C = 74C; DB/L = 222; DB/C = 22C; SGY/L = 132; SGN/L = 402; SB/L = 592.

**ABBREVIATIONS:** CM = Camel, CH = Charcoal, DR = Dark Red, DB = Dark Blue, SGY = Silver Gray, SGN = Silver Green, SB = Silver Beige, C = Cloth, L = Leather.

# 1984 CORVETTE
### Production: 51,547

## 1984 SERIAL NUMBERS

**Body and Chassis:** 1G1AY0781E5100001 thru 1G1AY0781E5151547
- Ninth digit is a check digit and varies

**Engine Suffix:** ZFD: 4-Speed     ZFF: Auto/Calif
               ZFC: Auto         ZFH: Export
               ZFN: 4-Speed/Calif

## 1984 FACTS

- The 1984 Corvette was a complete redesign in almost every aspect. Handling considerations dominated and the result was praised by the motoring press as the world's best cornering production automobile.

- Design criteria specified that the 1984 Corvette have more ground clearance and more interior headroom, but less overall height. In order to achieve this, engineers routed the exhaust system through the center tunnel at some expense to interior footwell room.

- Because of its late introduction in March 1983 and because the new Corvette met all 1984 Government requirements, Chevrolet decided to skip the 1983 model designation. 1983 Corvettes were built and serial numbered and the motoring press drove 1983's at the "long lead" press preview for the Corvette at Riverside Raceway in December 1982. But 1983 Corvettes were not released for sale to the public and officially 1983 Corvettes do not exist.

- In 1984, Corvettes were again available with four-speeds, but not early in production. The new Doug Nash units had automatically engaging overdrives in the top three gears specifically to avoid the Government "gas guzzler" tax.

- All 1984 Corvettes have one-piece liftoff tops and lifting rear hatch windows. The rear window glass was the largest compound glass ever installed in an American automobile and the front windshield was raked at the greatest angle (64°) of any American car.

- Brakes remained disc at all four wheels, but the components were new and included aluminum calipers supplied by Girlock of Australia.

- Electronic instrumentation was standard and included digital readouts for engine monitoring and liquid crystal graphic displays for speed and engine revolutions. Standard instruments were not available.

- The 1984 Corvette has a pad protruding from the passenger side of the dash. This was part of a passive restraint system designed when it was assumed the Government would require such restraints. The Reagan Administration dropped the restraint proposals, but the Corvette's pad remained.

- Weight of the 1984 Corvette was reduced about 250 pounds compared to 1982. Auto journalists expected a bigger drop and this was one of the few items criticized.

- The 1984 Corvette was designed to have no fiberglass seams on exposed panels that would require factory finishing. The exterior seams are under the rub strip extending around the entire car.

- A single transverse plastic leaf spring was used both front and rear.

• Chevrolet built specially modified 1984 Corvettes for the export markets of European, Middle East, Japanese and Latin American countries.

## 1984 OPTIONS

| RPO # | DESCRIPTION | UNITS* | RETAIL $ |
|---|---|---|---|
| 1YY07 | Corvette Sport Coupe | 51547 | 21800.00 |
| — | Leather Seats | 40568 | 400.00 |
| AG9 | Power Driver Seat | 48702 | 210.00 |
| AQ9 | Sport Seats | 4003 | 625.00 |
| AU3 | Power Door Locks | 49545 | 165.00 |
| CC3 | Removable Transparent Roof Panel | 15767 | 595.00 |
| D84 | Two-Tone Paint | 8755 | 428.00 |
| G92 | Performance Axle Ratio | 410 | 22.00 |
| KC4 | Engine Oil Cooler | 4295 | 158.00 |
| K34 | Cruise Control | 49832 | 185.00 |
| MM4 | Four-Speed Trans with Overdrives | 6443 | nc |
| QZD | Blackwall P255/50VR16 Tires/Wheels ** | 51547 | 561.20 |
| UM6 | Elect Tuned AM/FM Stereo Cassette | 6689 | 153.00 |
| UN8 | Elect Tuned AM/FM Stereo CB | 178 | 215.00 |
| UU8 | Delco/Bose Stereo System *** | 43607 | 895.00 |
| VO1 | Heavy Duty Radiator | 12008 | 57.00 |
| YF5 | California Emissions | 6833 | 75.00 |
| Z51 | Performance Handling Package **** | 25995 | 600.20 |
| Z6A | Defogger System | 47680 | 160.00 |

• Late introduction FG3 Bilstein shocks sold 3729 sets; UL5 radio delete selected 104 times.
*Sales during production year according to Chevrolet records.
**Includes special Goodyear tires mounted on 16-inch wheels.
***Includes AM/FM Stereo/Cassette with seek-scan, clock, special tone and balance controls and four Bose speakers.
****Includes special shock absorbers, springs, stabilizers and RPO QZD Goodyear Blackwall P255/50VR16 tires mounted on directional 16-inch wheels.

## 1984 COLORS

| CODE | EXTERIOR | SOFT TOP | WHEELS | INTERIORS GM SUGGESTED |
|---|---|---|---|---|
| 16 | Bright Silver | n/a | Alloy | GR, MG |
| 18 | Medium Gray | n/a | Alloy | GR, MG |
| 20 | Light Blue | n/a | Alloy | MB |
| 23 | Medium Blue | n/a | Alloy | MB |
| 72 | Bright Red | n/a | Alloy | GR, LS |
| 19 | Black | n/a | Alloy | GR, MG, LS, CA |
| 53 | Gold | n/a | Alloy | LS |
| 63 | Light Bronze | n/a | Alloy | DBR |
| 66 | Dark Bronze | n/a | Alloy | DBR |
| 10 | White | n/a | Alloy | GR, MG, MB, LS, DBR, CA |
| 16/18M | Silver/Gray | n/a | Alloy | GR, MG, |
| 20/23M | Lt Blue/Med Blue | n/a | Alloy | MB |
| 63/66M | Lt Bronze/Dk Bronze | n/a | Alloy | DBR |

• Additional color codes used: 70 and 33 for red, 41 for black, 40 for white.

**Interior Codes:** GR/L = 122; GR/C = 12C; GR/SC = 12V; MG/L = 152; MG/C = 15C; MG/SC = 15V; MB/C = 28C; MB/SC = 28V; LS/L = 622; LS/C = 62C; LS/SC = 62V; DBR/L = 652; DBR/C = 65C; DBR/SC = 65V; CA/L = 742.

ABBREVIATIONS: GR = Graphite, MG = Medium Gray, MB = Medium Blue, LS = Light Saddle, DBR = Dark Bronze, CA = Carmine, L = Leather, C = Cloth, SC = Sport-Seat-Cloth.

# 1985 CORVETTE

Production: 39,729

## 1985 SERIAL NUMBERS

Body and Chassis: 1G1YY0787F5100001 thru 1G1YY0787F5139729
• Ninth digit is a check digit and varies

Engine Suffix: ZDF: Auto w/o oil cooler     ZJJ: Auto w/oil cooler
ZJB: 4-Speed w/o oil cooler    ZJK: 4-Speed w/oil cooler
ZJC: Export

## 1985 FACTS

• Fuel injection returned to the Corvette in 1985 for the first time in two decades. The 1985 tuned port injection was standard equipment and featured a mass airflow sensor, aluminum tube-tuned intake runners, a mold-cast plenum, and an air cleaner mounted forward of the radiator support. This new L98 engine delivered a horsepower increase from 205 to 230, a torque increase from 290 pounds-feet to 330, and a fuel economy increase of 10%.

• Because of criticism of harsh ride quality in the 1984 Corvette, suspension rates were lowered for 1985. Springs for the standard suspension were softer by 26% in front and 25% in the rear. Springs for the optional Z51 suspension were 16% softer in front and 25% in the rear. Heavier anti-sway bars were added to the Z51 also.

• The RPO Z51 suspension option for 1985 included Delco/Bilstein shock absorbers and heavy duty cooling, but these options were available separately with standard suspensions as RPO FG3 and RPO V08 respectively.

• The overdrive selection switch for 4-speed manual transmissions was moved in interim 1985 to the gear shift knob from the console location.

• Electronic instrumentation continued in 1985 as the only style available, but displays were revised for better legibility.

• The optional Sport seat, available only in cloth for 1984, became available in leather for 1985 as a late option release.

• Exterior colors for 1985 remained as 1984, except the Bright Silver and Red were brighter hues.

• The bore of the brake master cylinder was increased in 1985 from 13/16″ to 7/8″, and the capacity of the power booster was increased. The booster itself was made of plastic, the first such application in an American car.

• A map strap was added to the 1985's driver-side sun visor.

• The RPO CC3 lift-off transparent roof panel was given stronger sun screening for 1985.

• Four-speed manual transmission 1985 models came with a new, heavy-duty 8½″ ring gear differential. Gearing for manual transmission 1985s was 3.07:1. Standard gearing for the automatics was 2.73:1, with the 3.07:1 optional as RPO G92.

• Wheel balancing weights were changed in 1985 from the standard outside rim clip-on style, to inner-surface adhesive style. The change was primarily for esthetics, but Chevrolet also claimed a better balance because of the adhesive weight's proximity to the wheel's depth center.

• The 1985 Corvette distributor was revised to prevent distributor spark ignition of exterior fuel vapors.

# 1985 OPTIONS

| RPO # | DESCRIPTION | UNITS* | RETAIL $ |
|-------|-------------|--------|----------|
| 1YY07 | Corvette Sport Coupe | 39729 | 24878.00 |
| A--2 | Leather Seats | 30955 | 400.00 |
| A--8 | Sport Seats, Leather | | 1025.00 |
| B--8 | Sport Seats, Cloth | 5661 | 625.00 |
| AG9 | Power Driver Seat | 37856 | 215.00 |
| AU3 | Power Door Locks | 38294 | 170.00 |
| CC3 | Removable Transparent Roof Panel | 28143 | 595.00 |
| D84 | Two-Tone Paint | 6033 | 428.00 |
| FG3 | Delco/Bilstein Shock Absorbers | 9333 | 189.00 |
| G92 | Performance Axle Ratio | 5447 | 22.00 |
| K34 | Cruise Control | 38369 | 185.00 |
| MM4 | Four-Speed Transmission with Overdrives | 9576 | n/c |
| NN5 | California Emissions | 6583 | 99.00 |
| UL5 | Radio Delete | 172 | -256.00 |
| UM6 | Elect Tuned AM/FM Stereo Cassette | 2958 | 122.00 |
| UN8 | Citizens Band Radio | 16 | 215.00 |
| UU8 | Delco-Bose Stereo System** | 35998 | 895.00 |
| V08 | Heavy Duty Cooling | 17539 | 225.00 |
| Z51 | Performance Handling Package*** | 14802 | 470.00 |
| Z6A | Defogger System | 37720 | 160.00 |

• Prices shown were introductory retail and included freight.
*Sales during production year according to Chevrolet records.
**Includes AM/FM Stereo/Cassette with seek-scan, clock, special tone and balance controls, and four Bose speakers.
***Includes RPO V08 heavy duty cooling, RPO FG3 Delco/Bilstein shock absorbers, heavy-duty front and rear springs, special wheels (9½"), and heavy-duty front and rear stabilizers.

# 1985 COLORS

| CODE | EXTERIOR | SOFT TOP | WHEELS | INTERIORS GM SUGGESTED |
|------|----------|----------|--------|------------------------|
| 13 | Silver | n/a | Alloy | GR, MG |
| 18 | Medium Gray | n/a | Alloy | GR, MG |
| 20 | Light Blue | n/a | Alloy | MB |
| 23 | Medium Blue | n/a | Alloy | MB |
| 40 | White | n/a | Alloy | MB, GR, MG, CA, LS |
| 41 | Black | n/a | Alloy | GR, MG, CA, LS |
| 53 | Gold | n/a | Alloy | LS |
| 63 | Light Bronze | n/a | Alloy | DBR |
| 66 | Dark Bronze | n/a | Alloy | DBR |
| 81 | Bright Red | n/a | Alloy | GR, MG, CA, LS |
| 13/18M | Silver/Gray | n/a | Alloy | GR, MG |
| 20/23M | Lt Blue/Med Blue | n/a | Alloy | MB |
| 63/66M | Lt Bronze/Dk Bronze | n/a | Alloy | DBR |

Interior Codes: GR/L = 122; GR/C = 12C; GR/SC = 12V; MG/L = 152; MG/C = 15C; MG/SC = 15V; MB/L = 282; MB/C = 28C; MB/SC = 28V; LS/L = 622; LS/C = 62C; LS/SC = 62V; DBR/L = 652; DBR/C = 65C; DBR/SC = 65V; CA/L = 742

ABBREVIATIONS: GR = Graphite, MG = Medium Gray, MB = Medium Blue, LS = Light Saddle, DBR = Dark Bronze, CA = Carmine, L = Leather, C = Cloth, SC = Sport Seat Cloth.

# 1986 CORVETTE

Production: 27,794 coupe, 7,315 convertible

## 1986 SERIAL NUMBERS

**Body and Chassis:** 1G1YY0789G5100001 thru 1G1YY0789G5127794
(coupes)
1G1YY6789G5900001 thru 1G1YY6789G5907315
(convertibles)
● Ninth digit is a check digit and varies

**Engine Suffix:**

DKF: Auto w/iron heads, w/KC4
DKC: Auto w/iron heads, w/o KC4
DKH: Auto w/iron heads, export
DKD: 4-spd w/iron heads, w/KC4
DKB: 4-spd w/iron heads, w/o KC4

ZJS: Auto w/alum heads, w/KC4
ZJH: Auto w/alum heads, w/o KC4
ZKD: Auto w/alum heads, export
ZJW: 4-spd w/alum heads, w/KC4
ZKA: 4-spd w/alum heads, w/o KC4

## 1986 FACTS

● The significant mechanical change for 1986 was the addition of anti-lock braking (ABS). An adaptation of Bosch's system, the Corvette's ABS featured rotational speed sensors at each wheel to feed data to a computerized Electronic Control Unit. Brake line pressure was then automatically distributed for optimum braking without wheel lockup and loss of steering control.

● A Corvette convertible model was reintroduced in interim 1986, the first Chevrolet-built Corvette convertible since the 1975 model.

● The 1986 Corvette convertible was the pace car for the 1986 Indy 500. All '86 model Corvette convertibles sold were designated as replicas.

● Aluminum cylinder heads were announced for 1986, but cracking around the head attachment bosses required a delay for design revisions. The heads were reintroduced in time for convertible production.

● All 1986 Corvettes featured centrally-located stoplamps to conform to federal legislation. The coupe's was mounted above the rear window; the convertible's in a less conspicuous rear facia location.

● All 1986 Corvettes received a VATS (Vehicle Anti-Theft System). It required a special ignition key with an embedded pellet. Lock cylinder contacts measured the pellet's electrical resistance and if correct (there were fifteen variations), the Corvette would start. If wrong, the Corvette wouldn't start and at least three minutes had to pass before another attempt be made.

● A removable hardtop for the convertible was not offered during 1986.

● Caster was changed in 1986 from four degrees to six degrees to improve on-center road feel and decrease wander.

● The 1986 steering wheel was redesigned with a thicker and softer rim section, and a different horn button.

● The standard Delco and the optional Delco-Bilstein shock absorbers for 1986 coupes were revalved. Convertibles got new Delco "deflected disc" shocks.

● The body of convertibles was 10-mm higher than coupes to maintain the same ground clearance under the convertible's additional chassis cross-bracing.

# 1986 OPTIONS

| RPO # | DESCRIPTION | UNITS* | RETAIL $ |
|-------|-------------|--------|----------|
| 1YY07 | Corvette Sport Coupe | 27794 | 27502.00 |
| 1YY67 | Corvette Convertible | 7315 | 32507.00 |
| A--2 | Leather Seats | — | 400.00 |
| A--8 | Sport Seats, Leather | 13372 | 1025.00 |
| AG9 | Power Driver Seat | 33983 | 225.00 |
| AU3 | Power Door Locks | 34215 | 175.00 |
| B4P | Radiator Boost Fan** | 8216 | 75.00 |
| B4Z | Custom Feature Package | 4832 | 195.00 |
| C2L | Dual Removable Roof Panels | 6242 | 895.00 |
| 24S | Removable Roof Panel-Blue Tint | 12021 | 595.00 |
| 64S | Removable Roof Panel-Bronze Tint | 7819 | 595.00 |
| C68 | Electronic Air Conditioning Control | 16646 | 150.00 |
| D84 | Two-Tone Paint | 3897 | 428.00 |
| FG3 | Delco-Bilstein Shock Absorbers** | 5521 | 189.00 |
| G92 | Performance Axle Ratio (3.07:1)** | 4879 | 22.00 |
| KC4 | Engine Oil Cooler** | 7394 | 110.00 |
| K34 | Cruise Control | 34197 | 185.00 |
| MM4 | Four-Speed Transmission with Overdrives | 6835 | n/c |
| NN5 | California Emissions | 5697 | 99.00 |
| UL5 | Radio Delete | 166 | 256.00 |
| UM6 | Elect Tuned AM-FM Stereo Cassette | 2039 | 122.00 |
| UU8 | Delco-Bose Stereo System | 32478 | 895.00 |
| VO1 | Heavy-Duty Radiator** | 10423 | 40.00 |
| Z51 | Performance Handling Package*** | 12821 | 470.00 |
| Z6A | Defogger System | 21837 | 165.00 |

• Prices shown were introductory retail and included freight.
*Sales during production year according to Chevrolet records.
**Included with RPO Z51.
***Includes RPO VO1, RPO B4P, RPO FG3, RPO KC4, heavy-duty front and rear springs, special wheels (9 1/2"), and heavy-duty front and rear stabilizers.

# 1986 COLORS

| CODE | EXTERIOR | SOFT TOP | WHEELS | INTERIORS GM SUGGESTED |
|------|----------|----------|--------|------------------------|
| 13 | Silver | Blk-W | Alloy | GR, MG |
| 18 | Medium Gray | Blk-W | Alloy | GR, MG, R |
| 20 | Medium Blue | Blk-W | Alloy | GR, B |
| 35 | Yellow | Blk-W | Alloy | GR |
| 40 | White | Blk-W-S | Alloy | GR, MG, R, B, BR, S |
| 41 | Black | Blk-W-S | Alloy | GR, MG, R, S |
| 53 | Gold | Blk-S | Alloy | GR, S |
| 59 | Silver Beige | Blk | Alloy | GR, BR |
| 69 | Medium Brown | S | Alloy | BR, S |
| 74 | Dark Red | Blk-W-S | Alloy | GR, S |
| 81 | Bright Red | Blk-W-S | Alloy | GR, R, S |
| 13/18 | Silver/Gray | n/a | Alloy | GR, MG, R |
| 18/41 | Gray/Black | n/a | Alloy | GR, MG |
| 40/13 | White/Silver | n/a | Alloy | GR, MG |
| 59/69 | Sil-Beige/Brown | n/a | Alloy | BR |

• The soft top availability shown was further limited for certain interior-exterior combinations.
**Interior Codes:** GR/L = 122; GR/C = 12C; MG/L =152; MG/C=15C; B/L=212; B/C = 21C; S/L = 622; S/C = 62C; BR/L = 652; BR/C = 65C; R/L = 732.
ABBREVIATIONS: GR = Graphite, MG = Medium Gray. B = Blue, S = Saddle, BR= Bronze, R = Red, Blk = Black, W = White, L = Leather, C = Cloth.

# 1987 CORVETTE

## 1987 SERIAL NUMBERS

**Body and Chassis:** 1G1YY2182H5100001 thru 1G1YY2182H51-----
- For convertibles, sixth digit is a 3.
- Ninth digit is a check digit and varies.

**Engine Suffix:** ZJN: Auto w/o KC4   ZLA: Auto w/KC4
      ZLC: 4-speed w/KC4   ZLB: Export
- For Callaway Twin-Turbo, see below.

## 1987 FACTS

- In appearance, the 1987 Corvette was similar to the 1986 model, but one visual difference between 1987 and earlier models was a change in wheel finish. The center sections of 1987 wheels were painted argent gray; 1986 wheel centers were not painted (the spoke openings were painted argent grey for both years). Center section and spoke openings of 1984 and 1985 wheels were painted black. Also, 1987 coupes came equipped with outside mirror air deflectors. In 1986, convertibles had the deflectors, coupes did not.

- The 350-cid engine with tuned-port fuel injection continued as the standard Corvette engine, but with roller valve lifters. The friction reduction attributed to the roller lifters resulted in a 3% increase in fuel economy and a power increase to 240-hp, up 5-hp from the 1986 aluminum-head motor.

- An optional engine package ($19,995) called the Callaway Twin Turbo was available through Chevrolet dealers as RPO B2K. The engines had street-legal emissions and the full Corvette warranty. Power was rated at 345-hp, torque at 465 lb.-ft @ 2800 rpm, top speed at 175 mph, and 0-60 mph at 4.6 seconds. Engines were built by Callaway Engineering at its Old Lyme, Connecticut shops starting with a replacement 350-cid 4-bolt mainbearing shortblock. Callaway stamped a nine-digit ID code into the blocks as follows: First two digits for year (87), next three digits for Callaway production sequence, last four digits to correspond to each car's regular Vehicle Identification Number (VIN).

- The overdrive-engage light moved from the center dash area of 1984-86 models to a more visible location within the tach display in 1987 models.

- The RPO Z51 performance handling package continued in 1987 with refinements. Some structural enhancements developed for the convertible were added to coupes with RPO Z51, and a power steering cooler was included. The RPO Z51 option required manual transmission and could not be ordered with convertibles.

- A new "sport" handling package (RPO Z52) became available in 1987 which combined elements of RPO Z51 with the softer suspension of the base models. Regular production option Z52 included RPO Z51 items like the RPO B4P radiator boost fan, RPO FG3 Bilstein shock absorbers, RPO KC4 oil cooler, RPO VO1 heavy-duty radiator, 9½" width wheels, faster 13:1 steering ratio, a larger front stabilizer bar on later production, and the convertible-inspired structural improvements for coupes. Available with automatic or 4-speed, coupe or convertible.

## 1987 OPTIONS

| RPO # | DESCRIPTION | UNITS* | RETAIL $ |
|-------|-------------|--------|----------|
| 1YY07 | Corvette Sport Coupe | — | 28,474.00 |
| 1YY67 | Corvette Convertible | — | 33,647.00 |
| A--2 | Leather Seats | — | 400.00 |
| A--8 | Sport Seats, Leather | — | 1,025.00 |
| AC1 | Power Passenger Seat | — | 240.00 |
| AC3 | Power Driver Seat | — | 240.00 |
| AU3 | Power Door Locks | — | 190.00 |
| B2K | Callaway Twin Turbo Engine | — | 19,995.00 |
| B4P | Radiator Boost Fan | — | 75.00 |
| C2L | Dual Removable Roof Panels | — | 915.00 |
| 24S | Removable Roof Panel—Blue Tint | — | 615.00 |
| 64S | Removable Roof Panel—Bronze Tint | — | 615.00 |
| C68 | Electronic Air Conditioning Control | — | 150.00 |
| DL8 | Twin Remote Heated Mirrors | — | 35.00 |
| D74 | Illuminated Driver Vanity Mirror | — | 58.00 |
| D84 | Two-Tone Paint | — | 428.00 |
| FG3 | Delco-Bilstein Shock Absorbers | — | 189.00 |
| G92 | Performance Axle Ratio (3.07:1) | — | 22.00 |
| KC4 | Engine Oil Cooler | — | 110.00 |
| K34 | Cruise Control | — | 185.00 |
| MM4 | Four-Speed Transmission with Overdrives | — | n/c |
| NN5 | California Emissions | — | 99.00 |
| UJ6 | Low Tire Pressure Indicator | — | 325.00 |
| UL5 | Radio Delete | — | -256.00 |
| UM6 | Elect-Tuned AM-FM Stereo Cassette | — | 132.00 |
| UU8 | Delco-Bose Stereo System | — | 905.00 |
| VO1 | Heavy-Duty Radiator | — | 40.00 |
| Z51 | Performance Handling Package | — | 795.00 |
| Z52 | Sport Handling Package | — | 470.00 |
| Z6A | Rear Window and Outside Mirror Defrosters | — | 165.00 |

·Prices shown were introductory and included freight.

## 1987 COLORS

| CODE | EXTERIOR | SOFT TOP | WHEELS | INTERIORS GM SUGGESTED |
|------|----------|----------|--------|------------------------|
| 13 | Silver | Blk-W | Alloy | GR, MG |
| 18 | Medium Gray | Blk-W | Alloy | GR, MG, R |
| 20 | Medium Blue | Blk-W | Alloy | GR, B |
| 35 | Yellow | Blk-W | Alloy | GR |
| 40 | White | Blk-W-S | Alloy | GR, MG, R, B, BR, S |
| 41 | Black | Blk-W-S | Alloy | GR, MG, R, S |
| 53 | Gold | Blk-S | Alloy | GR, S |
| 59 | Silver Beige | Blk | Alloy | GR, BR |
| 66 | Copper | Blk, S | Alloy | GR, S |
| 69 | Medium Brown | S | Alloy | BR, S |
| 74 | Dark Red | Blk-W-S | Alloy | GR, S |
| 81 | Bright Red | Blk-W-S | Alloy | GR, R, S |
| 13/18 | Silver/Gray | n/a | Alloy | GR, MG, R |
| 18/41 | Gray/Black | n/a | Alloy | GR, MG |
| 40/13 | White/Silver | n/a | Alloy | GR, MG |
| 59/69 | S-Beige/Brown | n/a | Alloy | BR |

● The soft-top availability shown was further limited for certain interior-exterior combinations.

Interior Codes: GR/L = 122; GR/C = 12C; MG/L = 152; MG/C = 15C; B/L = 212; B/C = 21C; S/L = 622; S/C = 62C; BR/L = 652; BR/C = 65C; R/L = 732.

ABBREVIATIONS; GR = Graphite, MG = Medium Gray, B = Blue, S = Saddle, BR = Bronze, R = Red, Blk = Black, W = White, L = Leather, C = Cloth.

# RIVER CITY
# CORVETTE PRINTS

The following Corvette illustrations (1953-1978) are reductions of River City art prints, hand-drawn by Leonard Kik. They are reproduced here with permission of the distributor, Mid-America Designs, Route 45 North, Effingham, Illinois 62401. (© 1975 River City). The prints may be purchased individually in their original size of 17½'' x 22½'' pre-matted from Mid-America. Order coupons are provided in the back of the Deluxe Corvette Black Book for your convenience.

1953                                      Production: 300

1954                                      Production: 3,640

1955

Production: 700

1956

Production: 3,467

1957

Production: 6,339

1958                                          Production: 9,168

1959                                          Production: 9,670

1960                                          Production: 10,261

*1961*

*Production: 10,939*

*1962*

*Production: 14,531*

*1963 Coupe*

*Production: 10,594*

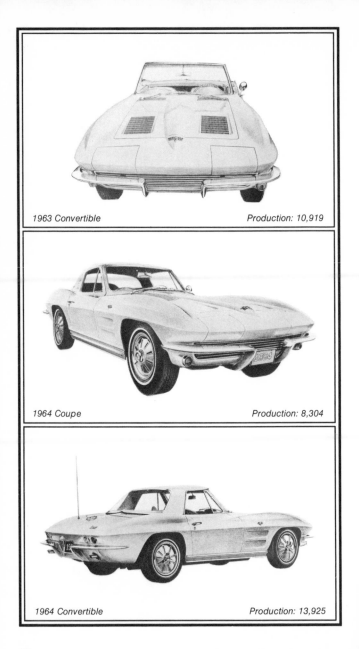

1963 Convertible       *Production: 10,919*

1964 Coupe       *Production: 8,304*

1964 Convertible       *Production: 13,925*

1965 Coupe                    Production: 8,186

1965 Convertible              Production: 15,376

1966 Coupe                    Production: 9,958

1966 Convertible                    Production: 17,762

1967 Coupe                          Production: 8,504

1967 Convertible                    Production: 14,436

1968 Coupe     *Production: 9,936*

1968 Convertible     *Production: 18,630*

1969 Coupe     *Production: 22,129*

*1969 Convertible*          *Production: 16,633*

*1970 Coupe*          *Production: 10,668*

*1970 Convertible*          *Production: 6,648*

1971 Coupe

Production: 14,680

1971 Convertible

Production: 7,121

1972 Coupe

Production: 20,496

1972 Convertible
Production: 6,508

1973 Coupe
Production: 25,521

1973 Convertible
Production: 4,943

1974 Coupe       *Production: 32,028*

1974 Convertible       *Production: 5,474*

1975 Coupe       *Production: 33,836*

1975 Convertible

Production: 4,629

1976 Coupe

Production: 46,558

1977 Coupe

Production: 49,213

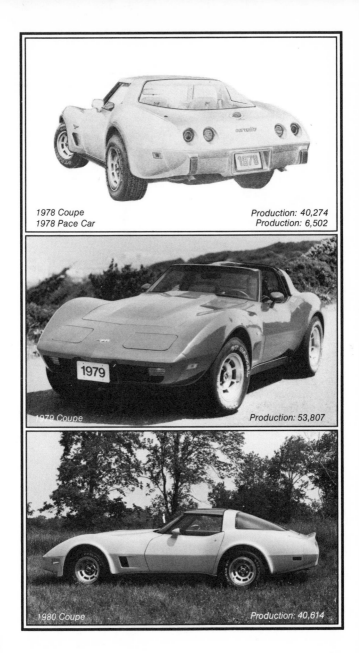

1978 Coupe
1978 Pace Car

Production: 40,274
Production: 6,502

1979 Coupe

Production: 53,807

1980 Coupe

Production: 40,614

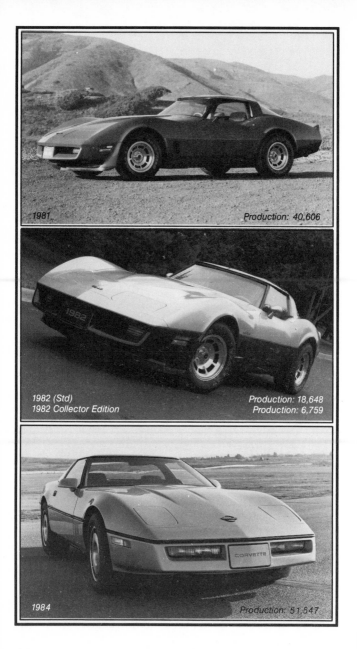

1981      Production: 40,606

1982 (Std)      Production: 18,648
1982 Collector Edition      Production: 6,759

1984      Production: 51,547

1985
Production: 39,729

1986 Coupe
1986 Convertible
Production: 27,794
Production: 7,315

1987

93

# CORVETTE LABELS

Corvettes can make no exclusive claim to the use of labels as owner-informative devices. Just where the practice of using labels (a term used loosely here to include also decals, tags, stickers, cards and other message-conveying materials) originated is anyone's guess. But thanks to its prodigious range of engine options, its variety of equipment, and its frequent use as a launch pad for new innovations, the Corvette seems to have attracted far more than its fair share.

A close look at the maze of things stuck onto Corvettes, from the radiator in front, to the gas filler in the rear, is interesting for two reasons. First, much can be learned about Corvettes by studying the information presented through the labels. The way the labels are worded, their purposes, and their appearance tell much about the Corvette's evolution from the six cylinder Blue Flame of the early years, to the beautiful highway cruisers of today. For this reason, reviewing the labels of all Corvettes can be fascinating to all owners, regardless of their own personal preferences.

More importantly, correct Corvette restoration requires an accurate understanding and proper use of labels. With just a few exceptions, labels used on Corvettes have not stood the test of time well. Many are paper and are subject to the effects of weather, engine heat, or just time. The more durable foil and plastic labels deteriorate eventually, no matter how carefully preserved. Worse, even those labels that have held up well are often destroyed or severely damaged during the restoration process. For instance, the metal or foil labels used for Harrison radiators are durable, but won't stand up to a radiator boil-out and refurbishing. Knowing what labels are required, knowing where to get them and how to use them, are indispensable for a good Corvette restoration.

Back in 1972, before Corvette restoration became the "in" thing, a gentleman named Murrell F. (Dob) Dobbins faced the problem of locating various labels to put the finishing touches to his 1967 model Corvette. A longtime Corvette buff, Dobbins knew what labels he needed, but not where to get them. The longer the search went on, the more difficult it became. In time, it became apparent that selling labels was something General Motors wasn't very interested in. Oh, a few could be purchased at Chevy parts counters, but for the most part, GM viewed labels as items to be put on during assembly, not sold later as replacement parts. Generally speaking, they just aren't necessary for the upkeep of an automobile, Corvettes included. And the more Dobbins looked, the more he realized that nobody else had much interest in providing Corvette labels either.

So Dobbins went about becoming his own source. He bought what was available through regular channels, and sought out the rest where he could. What wasn't available, he contracted to have reproduced. The rest of the story is as you might expect. Soon friends and even strangers approached him to get labels for their cars, too. It didn't take much analysis on Dob's part to figure out that this was a little corner of the Corvette market that no one else had staked out, so he might as well be the one.

In time, M. F. Dobbins became the master source of labels for the Corvette enthusiast. He now has available probably 95% of all the labels used for Corvettes from 1953 to the current year. He purchases what he can from General Motors for inventory. If it's simply not available anywhere, he'll contract to have it reproduced himself.

Along the way, Dobbins has by sheer osmosis, absorbed an awfully lot of knowledge about Corvette labels. In short, he's become a leading authority on the subject. There may be people who know a bit more about a particular year, but few can match Dob's knowledge of the entire range. So when it came to selecting someone to supply labels and expertise for an article of this type, Dob was the obvious choice.

Articles about Corvette labels have been done before. Dobbin's own books, **The Vette Vues Fact Book of the 1963-1967 Sting Ray**, and **The Vette Vues Fact Book of the 1968-1972 Stingray**, have excellent coverage of label usage on these models. The goal here is to present a really comprehensive look at the entire Corvette label spectrum. There are a couple of ways to organize such a presentation. The first would be chronological by model year. "The 1962 Corvette had a such and such label located on the rocker cover . . ." That technique has the advantage of being convenient for someone checking for a particular model, but the disadvantage of being somewhat difficult to follow when similar labels are used for several model years.

Another organization method would be to segregate labels by their purpose. There are labels which inform, such as the starting procedure label on the sunvisors of 1974 and 1975 Corvettes. There are labels which warn of danger, such as those affixed to air conditioning components cautioning of high refrigerant fluid pressures. There are labels which advertise or boast, like the "GM Mark of Excellence" aluminum stickers put on doors of '67 models, and the "Tonawanda No. 1 Team" valve cover labels. And there are those which simply adorn, like the "LT-1" hood labels.

A third way to segregate labels is by their location. Thus, categories would be divided into such group locations as air cleaner, valve cover, or radiator. The technique chosen to present this section actually combines all three choices. Overall divisions are roughly by location, but a chronological listing of years is presented within each location discussion. The purpose of each label is usually evident, but additional information relating to a label's intent is presented where appropriate. A "catch-all" category finishes off the article and includes all those labels which don't conveniently fit elsewhere.

Unfortunately, the nature of the inks, foil stocks, size, and fabrication techniques, prevent a genuinely accurate reproduction on this text's paper of all labels in their original form. Throughout the pictorial presentation, notes are included to indicate the coloration and material stock of each label, and the percentage of reduction of this text's representation relative to the original.

## Valve Covers

Valve covers have historically been Chevrolet's favorite location for advertising an engine's nickname, displacement, or horsepower. Such was the case with most Corvettes through the 1967. It started with the very first Corvettes made in Flint, the 1953 models.

**Above:** *1953 valve cover decals.* **Below:** *1954 valve cover decals. The lettering is white with red "speed" streaks. Shown 28% of actual size.*

The '53 Corvette's six cylinder valve cover was painted blue. This cover was a uniquely modified version of the passenger car's cover, and was attached by two central studs. To the valve covers were affixed water-activated decals (a decal or "decalcomania" is a water-activated label). On the right side (passenger side) appeared the words "Blue Flame" preceded by a small arrow pointed at the "B". The word "Special" was affixed to the left side (driver's side) of the valve cover, followed by a slightly skewed lightning bolt. The lightning bolt and all lettering were white, but the "Blue Flame" portion had red "speed" lines scattered through and between the lettering.

In 1954, the Corvette's valve cover changed (along with the Chevy passenger car) to a more smoothly shaped unit held down by four stovebolts around the periphery. The labels were again water activated decals, but changed in style. The "Blue Flame" and preceding small arrow were reduced in size from 1953, but were still put on the right hand side of the valve cover. This was followed by a "150" outlined by an arrow. Everything was again white, with red speed lines through the "Blue Flame" lettering. No decals were used on the left side of valve covers during 1954 Corvette production. Most valve covers of 1954 were painted blue, as in 1953, but some also appeared chromed. A running camshaft design change during 1954 lifted the horsepower of the Blue Flame Six from 150 to 155, but this was not reflected in a decal change as the "150" continued to be used throughout the year.

Also, some enthusiasts have assumed that the chrome valve covers which appeared during 1954 (and had no decals) were used for the higher horsepower engines. That may have been the intent, but it wasn't the result. The use of chrome valve covers in 1954 was random and did not coincide with engine horsepower, or anything else that has been determined.

The few 1955 model Corvettes built with six cylinder engines had the same valve cover decal treatment as the '54 models. No valve cover decals were used at all on the '55 V-8 models, which had chrome plated, stamped steel covers.

Decals weren't used on the painted steel valve covers of the base engines of 1956 or 1957 Corvettes, but it is generally believed that all optional engines had simple numerical decals indicating horsepower. Since the optional engines all had cast aluminum valve covers, Chevrolet selected "Chevy orange" as the decal color. The only engine option in 1956 was the dual-four carb package rated at 225 horsepower. The 1957, 245 HP engine continued on through 1961 with the same rating and same decals.

The 1957 Corvette had additional engines available at 250 horsepower (fuel injected), 270 horsepower (2x4 with special cam), and 283 horsepower (fuel injected with special cam). All received appropriate horsepower labels. The 270 horsepower engine carried through to 1961, but the fuel injected versions got power boosts. The 283 of 1957 became 290 horsepower in 1958 and 1959, then 315 for 1960 and 1961. The 250 horse fuel engine of 1957 continued at the same power rating through the 1959 model, then jumped to 275 horsepower in 1960 and 1961.

Decals for the base engine Corvettes of this period started appearing in 1958. Because the red decals used on the aluminum valve covers became visually lost on the orange-painted covers of the base engines, Chevy switched to gold, but only for the base engines. From 1958 through 1961, base Corvette engine horsepower remained at 230. Note that on Corvette V-8 engines built through the 1961 model year using valve cover decals, only one decal was used. It was always placed on the right hand valve cover.

1963 was the year of the big body and chassis change for the Corvette, but the step-up in engine displacement from 283 to 327 cubic inches occurred one model year earlier, in 1962. With the new engines came new valve cover decals.

To get away from two differently colored decals, Chevrolet came up with one that looked good on either cast aluminum or orange-painted surfaces. The new color scheme was metallic gold and black. Chevrolet also redesigned the painted steel valve covers for the lower horsepower engines. The new design eliminated the "Chevrolet" script previously used. In its place was a centrally located, rectangular recess into which was glued a label proclaiming, "Chevrolet 327 Turbo-Fire." This label was made of metal for the 1962 and early 1963 cars. Late in 1963, it was made of vinyl and remained vinyl through 1966. A small (3"x1") water-activated decal was placed about a half inch below the recess on the smooth valve cover surface. Where previous horsepower decals simply contained three numbers, the new style had the numbers and the word "horsepower" spelled out. Both the recess label and the horsepower decal were done in the metallic gold and black motif. Painted valve covers were used on the base 250 horsepower engine from 1962 through 1965, on the 300 horse

Valve cover decals used for Corvette V-8 engines (except 1955) through 1966. The top six are Chevy orange on clear. Others are black on metallic gold. Shown 46% of actual size.

engine available from 1962 through 1965 as an option, and on the same 300 engine which became the base powerplant in 1966. For the 300 horsepower engine in 1966, both labels were combined into a single label which read "327 Turbo-Fire 300 Horsepower."

The high horsepower, 327 cubic-inch displacement engines of the period had cast aluminum valve covers without the rectangular recesses, so they didn't get the "Chevrolet 327 Turbo-Fire" label, but similar gold and black horsepower decals were placed a half-inch below the last fin. Both the 340 and 360 horsepower motors of 1962 and 1963 have this treatment on their cast aluminum valve covers. The same is true of 1964 and 1965, though the horsepower ratings of these engines grew to 365 and 375 respectively. In 1965 and 1966, a 350 horsepower, 327 cubic-inch engine also joined the lineup and got similar valve cover decal treatment. The 350 horsepower engine also received the "Flint No. 1 Team" label on the front butt end of the right hand valve cover.

In 1967, strange things happened. On the base engine, 300 horsepower Corvettes, the same valve covers used prior to 1962 with the "Chevrolet" script were reintroduced. A red, white and blue paper label stating, "Flint No. 1 Team", was stuck onto the right side valve cover. The rear of the left side valve cover had a small yellow tag with a black number, probably an engine type indentifier. Engine size and horsepower labels for the small blocks moved to the air cleaners in 1967, so all such information was gone from valve covers.

Big block Corvettes came along in 1965, but not much use of their valve covers was made for decals. In the 1965, 396 cubic inch engine mill, no decals appeared on the valve covers at all. The same was true for the '66 model's 427 engines. The 1967 big blocks received a small, shiney "Built by Chevrolet Tonawanda THE NUMBER 1 TEAM" sticker on the right hand valve cover only. This continued through 1970 for all big blocks.

With the exception of a crossed-flag insignia, which barely qualifies as a label, the use of labels on valve covers petered out on Corvettes around 1970. The reasons are fairly obvious. Corvette engine compartments were becoming cluttered with a maze of paraphernalia required by not only a sharp increase in preference for highly optioned Corvettes, but by an ever-increasing degree of plumbing required to meet federal emission standards. It was getting difficult to see the valve covers, let alone labels attached. So Chevrolet moved engine information labels up where they could be seen, to the top surface of the air cleaners.

# Air Cleaners

It doesn't take a great deal of savvy to understand what to do with an air cleaner element. It either gets pitched out and replaced with a new one, or it gets cleaned. Other than the appropriate instructions in owner's manuals, Chevrolet hasn't seen the necessity to go into much detail about air cleaner instructions via the label route. On later models, Chevrolet did use the top of the air cleaner for engine information, since the air cleaner offered a nice, unobstructed viewing surface.

Exceptions to the use of air cleaner decals did occur for fuel injected Corvettes, for two reasons. First, fuel injection was a strange looking critter to someone used to seeing carburetors. Especially with the '63 and later units, it wasn't all that evident to the novice that there even was an air cleaner

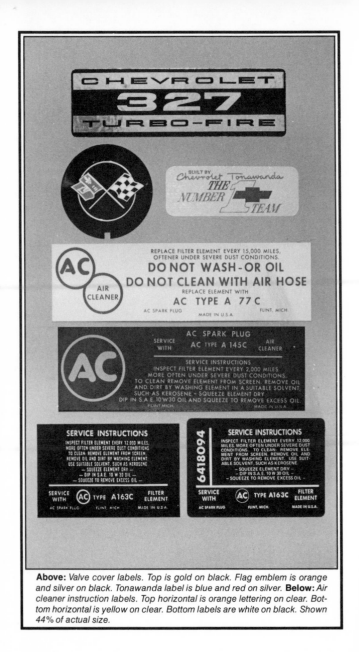

**Above:** Valve cover labels. Top is gold on black. Flag emblem is orange and silver on black. Tonawanda label is blue and red on silver. **Below:** Air cleaner instruction labels. Top horizontal is orange lettering on clear. Bottom horizontal is yellow on clear. Bottom labels are white on black. Shown 44% of actual size.

*Air cleaner horsepower and displacement labels for Corvette "small" block V-8 engines, used from 1967 through 1971. All are orange on silver. Shown 22% of actual size.*

*Air cleaner horsepower and displacement labels. Flag label centers above one horsepower band. Flag labels are orange, white, and black on silver. Curved bands are orange on silver. Shown 28% of actual size.*

in that big black tube. More importantly, fuel injection is valuable and somewhat sensitive equipment. Chevy felt the need to inform owners clearly that the units needed a clean, unobstructed air source.

The '57 Corvette with fuel injection had an air cleaner element, which was disposable, attached close to the injection unit. The filtering unit was exposed, and replacement time made itself pretty well known. No decal was used. But the 1958 through 1962 Corvettes had fender-mounted air cleaners for fuel units, and it was with these units that Chevy saw the necessity of using decals on the cleaner to specify proper care. For the 1958 through 1961 models, this took the form of an orange decal placed right on top of the air cleaner. It specified that the filter element should be replaced every 15,000 miles, "oftener" under severe dust conditions. It cautioned not to attempt to clean by washing, oiling, or air blasting. A type A-77C filter (AC, natch) was the recommended replacement.

The filter element of the fuel injected '62 model Corvettes changed, so the decal did, too. Instead of orange, it was yellow. And the instructions were completely different, since the '62 element was a re-usable type that was to be inspected every 2,000 miles, cleaned in a "suitable solvent" such as kerosene, and oiled with 10W30 motor oil. It was placed on the air cleaner, next to the fender bracket. The decal was close in size to that used the previous four model years.

The air cleaner and element changed again in 1963, and Chevy started using a small black vinyl label with white lettering. Its instructions were similar to that of 1962, since the element was again the re-usable type. The same label was used for 1963 and 1964 fuel injected Corvettes, but was revised slightly in 1965. Considering that '65 was fuel injection's last year, it's strange that Chevy would bother to change the decal, since the instructions and replacement element (AC type A163C) remained the same. The only changes to the '65 decal were rounded corners, more legible type style with instructions spread over six lines instead of five, and the addition of a part number.

1967 marked the start of the use of labels on the top of the carburetor air cleaners of small block Corvettes to designate engine displacement and horsepower. The two 327 cubic inch displacement engines which had horsepower ratings of 300 and 350, had red labels on silver adhesive paper stock. The type was in three curved lines reading "327" on the first line, TURBO-FIRE on the second line, and either 300 or 350 HORSEPOWER on the third. The 1968 small block engines had the same power ratings, and used the very same labels. In 1969, Corvette engine displacement for the small blocks increased to 350 cubic inches. For both 1969 and 1970, similar air cleaner decals were used as for '67 and '68, with the appropriate changes in displacement and horsepower. Both '69 and '70 had small block engines with 300 and 350 horsepower, and 1970 also saw the introduction of the LT-1, rated at 370 horses. The LT-1 of 1970 was the highest rated, non-fuel injected small block ever available in a Corvette, and it lasted only a year in its high-horsepower form.

For the 1971 model year, General Motors detuned its engines to permit using regular and no-lead fuels, allowing fuel companies to start phasing in the unleaded gas needed for catalytic converters, which everyone knew were coming in a few years. The '71 base engine became 270 horsepower, and the

*Air cleaner horsepower and displacement labels for "454" engine Corvettes. Black and white on silver. Shown 29% of actual size.*

LT-1 dropped to 330, thanks to lower compression ratios. Again, the same type of labels on the air cleaners were used.

In 1972, horsepower ratings dropped again, this time a result of the technique used to determine power, not because of any major engine change. Still, a rating of 255 horsepower, compared to the rating of 370 for the engine just two years earlier, was something Chevy chose not to brag about. Starting in 1972, displacement and power ratings disappeared from Corvette air cleaners.

The "big block" engines of the 1965 through 1971 period also used air cleaner labels to proclaim displacement and power ratings. These labels were also of the paper-foil adhesive-backed type, but styles varied. The 1965 big engine had a red, white, black, grey, and silver label which incorporated the Corvette crossed-flag emblem and the numerals, "396". Below this label was placed a curved band in red and silver, which stated, "TURBO-JET 425 HP". The 425 horsepower engine of 1966 got the same labels, except that the "396" became "427" to reflect the increase in displacement. Variations of the same labels were also used for the 390 horsepower versions of the 427 engines for 1966, '67, '68, and 1969.

The big blocks of the 1967 through 1969 period which used triple carbs were treated to unique labels. These combined the crossed flag emblem with a lower section that read, "TURBO-JET 427 3x2 435 HORSEPOWER" (or

400 HORSEPOWER). The colors were red, white, black, silver, and grey. These were again the foil paper, adhesive-backed type.

1970 through 1974 Corvettes had as options the largest engines ever, displacement wise. The big block was opened up to 454 cubes. Power ratings in 1970 were 460 and 390 horsepower, and each got label treatment similar to '65-69 Corvette big engines, with obvious numerical corrections. Horsepower ratings dropped in 1971 to 425 and 365 respectfully, and each engine got an all-new larger silver, white, and black air cleaner label which indicated displacement and power.

Starting in 1971, all engines (except the '71 and '72 LT-1) started receiving a small paper label on the air cleaner which advised the owner to "Keep your GM car all GM". These labels were printed in red, white, and varying shades of blue. There are at least six different versions used. All show GM, Delco, and "AC" trademarks and all (except 1971) list the correct air filter replacement number. The labels changed each year as far as part number, but not necessarily other information. The labels used in 1972, for instance, contain the same information as those used in 1973. But the 1972 labels are slightly smaller, have a different part number, and use a brighter shade of blue ink. 1974 through 1976 labels look exactly the same, but the part number for each is different. If the label on your Corvette is intact, get every bit of information from it before ordering a replacement. Then compare the replacement to the original. It seems a minor point, but Corvette people are in a world of their own when it comes to accuracy and originality.

## Jacking Instructions

Jacking instructions for Corvettes have always been paper labels, placed in locations conspicuous when retrieving either the jack or the spare tire.

Chevrolet made good use of the jack instructions label developed for the first Corvettes. A label was attached to the plywood spare tire compartment cover, and showed sketches of the 1953-1955 Corvette hubcap. Despite the sketch, and the instructions to "set parking brake, move selector lever to park position . . .", which obviously applied to the automatic transmission installed in all 1953 and 1954 Corvettes, the label continued to be used for all Corvettes through the 1960 model.

A completely new label was designed for the 1961 and 1962 models. The problem of instructions for manual transmissions was solved by recommending leaving the gearshift in reverse for jacking rear wheels, and in "first" when jacking the front wheels. The label was much larger, with illustrations of front and rear jacking techniques, tire stowage details, and a sample situation sketch showing a '61 model jacked at the right rear and blocked at the left front.

1962 was the last year for a rear-access trunk in Corvettes. In 1963, the spare tire was moved to a special hinged tray, below the rear of the car. The tray is held in place by a sliding bolt arrangement, the bolt head conveniently being the same size as the wheel lug bolts so that the lug wrench can be used to loosen the retaining bolt. Access requires working on one's knees, or even flat on the back, and many a Corvette owner has had unpleasant comments about the difficulty of getting at the spare tire.

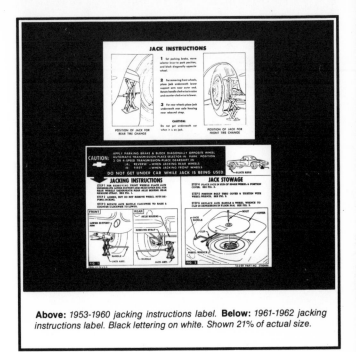

**Above:** *1953-1960 jacking instructions label.* **Below:** *1961-1962 jacking instructions label. Black lettering on white. Shown 21% of actual size.*

The new spare location in 1963 required a completely new instructions label. The label was pasted to the inside of the carpet-covered masonite storage compartment behind the seats (except in 36.5 gallon fuel tank cars), which housed the jack and lug wrench. The same label was used from 1963 through 1966, except that Corvettes with knock-off aluminum wheels had a modified version. The knock-off wheel label was the same size and contained the same sketches, except that one sketch had the knock-off spinners roughed in and the lead hammer used to remove the wheels shown in place of the jack. In addition to the obvious instruction required for "striking the spinner a sharp blow...", the knock-off label had far more detailed things to say about removing the spare and replacing it. Remember that contrary to the current practice of supplying only four aluminum wheels with new Corvettes, the option price in 1963 through 1967 included all five. The knock-off label for 1963-1966 went so far as to specify proper torque for the spare tire retaining cover bolt. Chevrolet wanted them to stay put. In Corvettes equipped with the 36.5 gallon fuel tank, the jacking instructions label was placed in the rear corner, top left side of the tank cover.

Safety standards required the knock-off wheel of the 1963-1966 period to be changed in 1967 to a design without spinners. This completely new wheel was a bolt-on style, with a center cap to hide lug nuts. This new wheel option required a new jacking instruction label, though the old label would have

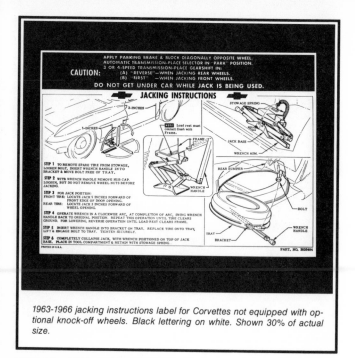

*1963-1966 jacking instructions label for Corvettes not equipped with optional knock-off wheels. Black lettering on white. Shown 30% of actual size.*

sufficed for '67 Corvettes with the newly-standard rally wheel treatment. Despite that, Chevrolet decided to re-do the label completely, again. For 1967, they came up with a much smaller (less than half size) label than used for previous Sting Rays. The new label was worded to cover either type of wheel installed, "WITH ALUMINUM WHEELS, USE SCREW DRIVER TO REMOVE COVER ASM", and the previously elaborate instructions for putting the spare back in place were left out completely. Chevrolet must have figured that if you were smart enough to get the spare out, you'd get it back in.

Bolt-on aluminum wheels were gone as an option in 1968, and this year brought on a completely new body style. The chassis of the 1968 Corvette was virtually the same as the previous five years, and the spare remained in the same location, as it has through current models. A new jacking instructions label was again designed for 1968, and the label remained unchanged through 1972. Someone in Chevrolet must have been preaching either paper savings, or simplicity, because this label got even smaller than 1967's, and instructions were at an absolute minimum. Gone were the details about what gear to leave the Corvette in while jacking, and it took real concentration to figure the tire tray illustration out. Heaven have mercy on he or she who was doing this for the first time!

The jacking label made a complete about-face in 1973. The label grew to more than double-size. All previous jacking instruction labels had been black

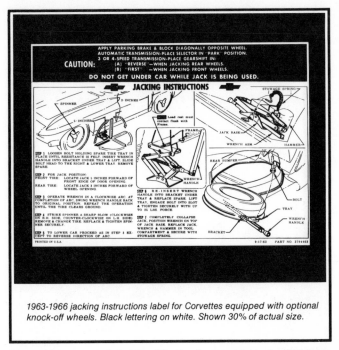

*1963-1966 jacking instructions label for Corvettes equipped with optional knock-off wheels. Black lettering on white. Shown 30% of actual size.*

ink on white paper stock, but four "Cautions" were added to the '73 label in red ink:

(1) REFER TO OWNER'S MANUAL AND FOLLOW JACKING PREPARATION AND INSTRUCTIONS IN ORDER TO REDUCE THE POSSIBILITY OF SERIOUS INJURY.

(2) THE JACK IS DESIGNED FOR USE ONLY WHEN CHANGING WHEELS.

(3) NEVER GET BENEATH THE VEHICLE WHEN IT IS SUPPORTED ONLY BY A JACK

(4) DO NOT START OR RUN ENGINE WHILE VEHICLE IS ON JACK.

The instructions concerning proper transmission gear while jacking returned. For the first time, mention was made of engaging the four-way flasher system while changing tires, even though the flashers had been standard on Corvettes since the 1967 model. Only two sketches were used, but they were well detailed. Since the jack was hidden under an insert tray in one of three compartments behind the seats, this was included in the illustration.

In 1975, the label was updated again, resulting in probably the clearest and most complete jacking instructions label ever. Illustrations were similar, but sharper. The cautions were reworded slightly and printed in yellow instead of red. Instructions were expanded, but listed in an easy-to-follow group of nine numbered statements. Unlike every other jacking label used for Corvettes, the title of this label was "Jack Usage".

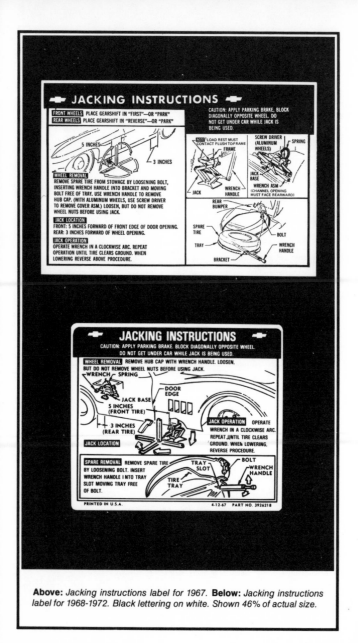

**Above:** *Jacking instructions label for 1967.* **Below:** *Jacking instructions label for 1968-1972. Black lettering on white. Shown 46% of actual size.*

**Above:** *1973-1974 jacking instructions label.* **Below:** *1975-1978 jacking instructions label. Black lettering on white, except for "caution" which is red on top label and yellow on bottom. Shown 23% of actual size.*

The return to detailed, comprehensive jacking labels on later model Corvettes parallels a national concern for safety. In the case of the Corvette specifically, it probably also reflects an awareness on the part of Chevrolet that its later Corvettes were appealing to and being purchased by a much more diverse group of people whose mechanical know-how could no longer be taken for granted.

## Radiator and Cooling System

Though there is some question as to the consistency of usage, GM assembly drawings indicate that labels started to be applied to the radiators of Corvettes starting with the 1954 model. The first label used was a simple and small, green on white paper caution that read, "THIS COOLANT SYSTEM PROTECTED TO −20° FAHRENHEIT BY GM PERMANENT TYPE ANTI-FREEZE."

In 1958, a larger label replaced the '55-57 one. It was again green on white, but the message changed. The new label stated that the engine was equipped with a 170° thermostat and was designed to operate on permanent type (ethylene glycol base) anti-freeze only. If non-permanent type were used, the label recommended changing the thermostat to 160° or less. This same label was used from 1958 through 1962, but the location changed. The 1958 through 1960 models, and the '61 with integral expansion tank

## CAUTION

THIS COOLANT SYSTEM
PROTECTED TO −20°
FAHRENHEIT BY
GM PERMANENT
TYPE ANTIFREEZE

## CAUTION

THIS ENGINE IS EQUIPPED WITH 170 F. THERMOSTAT
AND IS DESIGNED TO OPERATE ON PERMANENT
TYPE (ETHYLENE GLYCOL BASE) ANTI-FREEZE ONLY.
IF **NON-PERMANENT** TYPE (METHANOL BASE) IS USED,
THE THERMOSTAT MUST BE CHANGED TO 160 F. OR LESS.

## CAUTION

THIS ENGINE IS EQUIPPED WITH 180°F THERMOSTAT
AND IS DESIGNED TO OPERATE ON PERMANENT TYPE
(ETHYLENE GLYCOL BASE) ANTI- FREEZE ONLY.
IF NON-PERMANENT TYPE (METHANOL BASE) IS USED,
THE THERMOSTAT MUST BE CHANGED TO 160°F OR LESS

## CAUTION
FILLER CAP MUST BE TIGHT
THIS ENGINE IS EQUIPPED WITH 180° THERMOSTAT
AND IS DESIGNED TO OPERATE ON PERMANENT TYPE
(ETHYLENE GLYCOL BASE) ANTI-FREEZE ONLY.
METHANOL BASE (ALCOHOL) COOLANTS ARE NOT
RECOMMENDED FOR THIS VEHICLE. SEE OWNERS MANUAL.

COOLING SYSTEM WAS PROTECTED TO − 20°F, AT TIME OF DELIVERY FROM PLANT.
CAUTION  USE PERMANENT TYPE (ETHYLENE GLYCOL BASE) ANTI-FREEZE ONLY.
METHANOL BASE (ALCOHOL) NOT RECOMMENDED FOR THIS VEHICLE.

COOLING SYSTEM IS EQUIPPED WITH 180° THERMOSTAT AND IS PRESSURIZED.
CAUTION  ALWAYS BE SURE RADIATOR CAP IS INSTALLED TIGHTLY OTHERWISE
DAMAGE TO ENGINE MAY RESULT FROM OVER-HEATING.
SEE OWNERS GUIDE FOR SERVICE RECOMMENDATIONS

*Radiator caution labels. See text for correct applications. Lettering is green on white. Shown 56% of actual size.*

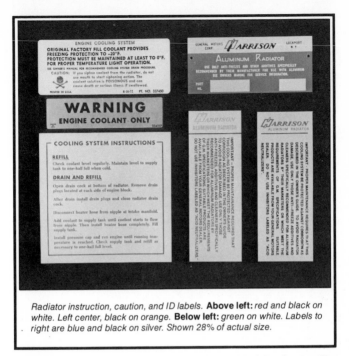

*Radiator instruction, caution, and ID labels. **Above left:** red and black on white. Left center, black on orange. **Below left:** green on white. Labels to right are blue and black on silver. Shown 28% of actual size.*

radiator, had the label on top of the radiator just to the right of center. The 1961 models with supply tanks and all '62 Corvettes had the label on the top left side of the radiator.

Starting with the 1960 high horsepower small blocks (270 hp, 315 hp), Chevy began using aluminum radiators in Corvettes. Those '60 models with aluminum radiators, and the early '61's, had the integrated overflow tank built right into the top of the radiator. On these models, an aluminum plate with blue and black printing was screwed to the expansion tank or the radiator. This tag also appeared on early '62 models. All the other '61 and newer small block Corvettes had aluminum radiators with fender-mounted expansion tanks. These received a silver foil radiator label (adhesive backed) through 1968, except for late '62 and early '63, when an adhesive-backed plate was used. To keep things really confusing, the little green tag that appeared on '55 and '57 radiators surfaced again, this time below the expansion tank neck of '61 and '62 Corvettes so equipped.

New green on white paper caution labels started to be used on the '63 model, but the first version was revised quickly and was used only for '63 Corvettes built before December, 1962. The early version still had the comment about switching the thermostat to a lower temperature type if non-permanent type (methanol base) anti-freeze was used. On the revised '63 label, Chevrolet flat-out told owners not to use anything but permanent

111

anti-freeze. This label was used through the remainder of the '63 model run and into 1964 (up until April of 1964 in fact), when it changed again. Additions included a new warning about possible engine damage from overheating due to an improperly tightened radiator cap, and a notation that the system was factory-protected to −20°F. This label continued in use through 1965 and possibly into 1966.

The three green and white radiator/cooling system labels for the '63 through '65 models were not placed in the same locations. The first, that one appearing on just early '63 cars, went on the side of the supply tank, facing the rear of the car. Its replacement, the one used for the remainder of 1963 and part of 1964, went on the top left side of the radiator. Some 1963 cars are known to have both labels from the factory. The third was put on the right side of the radiator shroud, reading from bottom to top in about the one-two o'clock position.

With the exception of the 396 and L-88, big block radiators were made of copper, so they did not use the Harrison aluminum radiator labels. The 396 cubic inch '65 models did have a large, green on white paper label affixed to their fender walls which explained the correct procedure for draining and refilling the radiator. The '66 and '67 big block models did not use radiator expansion tanks, and did not have the big green tags. The '65 big block also had the long green on white "caution" label on its radiator shroud used the same year on small block equipped cars.

Use of labels for later model Corvettes has been somewhat sporadic. The '73 Corvettes had a unique red and black on white paper label that had a caution, complete with skull and crossbones, concerning not using your mouth to siphon coolant from the radiator. The '74 through '77 models had a "WARNING... ENGINE COOLANT ONLY" sticker on the plastic expansion tanks to keep unknowing station attendants from pouring oil or power steering fluid in. 1963 and newer Corvettes often have small numeral decals on the cooling system components which are presumably inspection numbers. The radiator cap on the expansion tank of the 1978-1982 models had a round label which read "Notice engine coolant only." Fan shrouds for the 1979-80 and 1981-82 models had black and yellow fan caution labels.

# Air Conditioning

The first year for factory-installed air conditioning in Corvettes was 1963, and that's when the label story starts, too. The '63 equipped with air had a unique red on white caution label inside the glove box. This label instructed the owner to run the air conditioning unit five minutes each week during the off season to keep the system in "good" condition. No such label appeared on any later model Corvettes.

The '63 through '66 Corvettes equipped with air had blue Chevrolet "bow tie" emblems with "air conditioning" spelled out. The '63 through '65 version had the lettering within the bow tie, but for '66 the lettering was below. These labels were placed on the rear corner of the passenger-side of the rear window of coupes, and on the passenger-side roll-up window of convertibles.

Several labels were used within the engine compartment for air conditioned Corvettes. The '64 to '65 models had a black on silver foil "Frigidaire" label placed on the back end of the compressor. They were put on so that they could be read from the "mechanic's angle" front of the car.

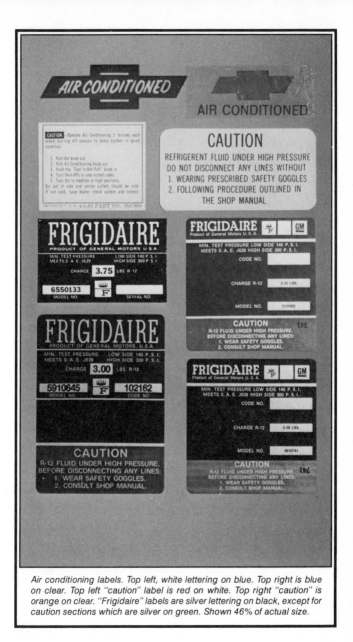

*Air conditioning labels. Top left, white lettering on blue. Top right is blue on clear. Top left "caution" label is red on white. Top right "caution" is orange on clear. "Frigidaire" labels are silver lettering on black, except for caution sections which are silver on green. Shown 46% of actual size.*

*Harrison air conditioning labels. All are blue and black on silver. Shown 46% of actual size.*

Another label used for the same models was an orange decal cautioning of high pressure lines. This went on the pulley end of the compressor top. A third label used was made of sheet aluminum and was stuck to the exchanger box with adhesive. This "Harrison" air conditioning label identified model, year, and serial numbers of the unit. During 1964 production, the material of the label changed from sheet aluminum to thinner foil stock. But the appearance of the label and the information on it was similar, though '65 through '67 versions of the label did not include the serial numbers.

In 1966, the "Frigidaire" and "caution" labels used the previous years were combined in one new label. The Frigidaire ID portion was again black on silver, but the caution part became green. This label continued in this exact form through the 1969 model. Similar labels, reduced in size, appeared on later Corvettes, also. The "Harrison" air conditioning heat exchanger label also continued on Corvettes to current years, but each finished label is unique to the year since each model year is designated.

## Glove Box, Door, And Sun Visor Labels

It was in 1958 that Corvettes made the complete change to acrylic lacquer for exterior finishes. Starting in 1958, and continuing through 1961, Chevrolet put a warning label into the lid of the glove box to inform owners that the new lacquer being used was not compatible with enamels or other lacquers. However, early in 1958 production, this red and white label was put on the top of the fan shroud. Also, a few 1957 models were painted silver, and that particular silver was acrylic lacquer. These models had the same red and white paint warning label, but it was placed on the firewall, above the heater.

1966 was the first year that Chevrolet informed Corvette owners of recommended tire pressures through labels. This was done with an adhesive-backed, round label placed on the inside surface of the glove box door. The 1967 model's label contained the exact same information (24 pounds of air pressure in all tires cold, 30 hot), but for some reason a new part number was assigned to it. For 1968 through 1972 Corvettes, another tire pressure label was designed, this time a bit larger, but with the same recommendations.

Tire pressure labels moved to the door posts starting in 1973. The label for 1973 to 1975 Corvettes is square, as are following years. The '73-'75 recommends 20 pounds of pressure for both front and rear tires at cold temperatures. This changed in 1976 to a recommendation of 26 pounds rear and 20 pounds front.

A really unusual label appeared on the doors of 1967 Corvettes, and on all other General Motors cars of the era. GM management had decided a drive for improved quality was in order, and one of the visual outgrowths of that program was the adoption of a "GM Mark of Excellence" trademark. This neat logo started showing up everywhere, including a bright blue and silver stick-on label for Corvette doors. The logo continued for years, but the door stickers just lasted one model year.

Another one year item was a gasoline recommendation label applied to the center storage compartment of 1973 models. This little paper sticker advised owners that 91 Research Octane fuel was all that was needed, and buying better was an "unnecessary additional expense."

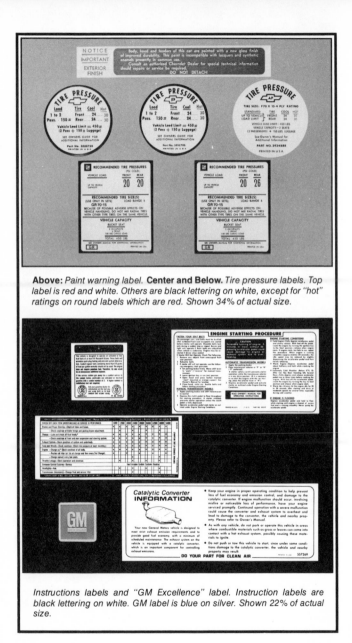

**Above:** *Paint warning label.* **Center and Below.** *Tire pressure labels. Top label is red and white. Others are black lettering on white, except for "hot" ratings on round labels which are red. Shown 34% of actual size.*

*Instructions labels and "GM Excellence" label. Instruction labels are black lettering on white. GM label is blue on silver. Shown 22% of actual size.*

Sun visors haven't been the most popular place for labels, but the Corvette had seen a couple of instances of its use for that purpose. The first was in 1969 when a three color paper sheath label was slid onto the driver's visor. On one side the new steering ignition lock system was explained and on the other side the starting procedure was described. A first design was dated August 1968 and a second design was dated October 1968. The second was in 1971 when a black and white fiberglass "maintenance" schedule was placed on the inside surface of the driver's visor. The same schedule was used the following year, but the label for it was paper and it was moved to the center of the storage compartment.

A third use of the visor for labels came in 1976 when a catalytic converter information label was affixed to the passenger visor. This label had the usual business about keeping the engine in good tune, but also stated, "As with any vehicle, do not park or operate this vehicle in areas where combustible materials such as grass or leaves can come in contact with a hot exhaust system, possibly causing these materials to ignite." What GM was hinting at, but not coming right out and saying, was that converters got very hot. They got so hot that they could catch dried leaves and such on fire if you parked over them. In fact, many national and state parks prohibit catalytic converter-equipped cars to park in certain areas for fear of starting forest fires.

In 1974 and 1975, an engine starting procedure label was placed on the sun visor. This was the era of the infamous "interlock" seat belt system which required the driver and passenger (or a package in the passenger seat of over a few pounds) to be buckled up before the car would start. There was a by-pass button under the hood to be used if the system fouled, and the confusion of it all led Chevrolet to go with a detailed explanation via the visor label.

# Emissions

The 1968 model year brought with it the beginning vestiges of emissions control equipment. Appropriate labels for the engine compartment came with this equipment. They told of its presence and how to tune-up the engine in spite of it. The first year (1968) the labels were long and narrow and printed in red and black on white adhesive paper stock. They were placed on the top left side of the radiator. A different label was used for each engine (one was used for the 390 hp and 400 hp), and the 300 hp engine with automatic had a different label than the 300 hp with manual transmission, because the timing and RPM settings were different. Each label had its own separate part number and letter suffix on the right hand side.

From 1969 on, the labels were placed on the firewall above the brake master cylinder. Placement on the radiator may not have been good because of road dirt, heat, and antifreeze.

The 1969 and 1970 labels were printed in the same colors and on the same stock as the 1968 labels, but each year had a different layout for the information.

In 1971 a few changes occurred in the emission labels. They were made larger to accommodate more information and printed in black only on white stock. In order to withstand abuse better, the labels were laminated with clear plastic. The labels have basically remained the same, except for a reduction in

**THIS ENGINE IS EQUIPPED TO REDUCE EXHAUST EMISSIONS**

THE FOLLOWING ADJUSTMENTS ARE NECESSARY TO MAINTAIN THE EFFECTIVENESS OF THE SYSTEM
(With engine at operating temperature, choke open, air cleaner installed, air conditioning on.)
1. Set mixture screw(s) for max. idle rpm and adjust speed screw to obtain **700 RPM IN NEUTRAL.**
2. Set ignition timing at 4° BTC (Plug vacuum advance line — this step only.)
3. Adjust mixture screw in to obtain a 20 rpm drop (lean roll.)
4. Adjust mixture screw out 1/4 turn.
5. Repeat steps 3 and 4 for second mixture screw (if so equipped.)
6. Readjust speed screw if necessary to specified idle rpm.
See Service Manual for Additional Tune-Up Instruction.     PRINTED IN U.S.A.

PART NO. 3932390     T

**THIS ENGINE IS EQUIPPED TO REDUCE EXHAUST EMISSIONS**

THE FOLLOWING ADJUSTMENTS ARE NECESSARY TO MAINTAIN THE EFFECTIVENESS OF THE SYSTEM
(With engine at operating temperature, choke open, air cleaner installed, air conditioning off.)
1. Set mixture screw(s) for max. idle rpm and adjust speed screw to obtain **750 RPM IN NEUTRAL.**
2. Set ignition timing at 4° BTC (Plug vacuum advance line — this step only.)
3. Adjust mixture screw in to obtain a 20 rpm drop (less roll.)
4. Adjust mixture screw out 1/4 turn.
5. Repeat steps 3 and 4 for second mixture screw (if so equipped.)
6. Readjust speed screw if necessary to specified idle rpm.
See Service Manual for Additional Tune-Up Instruction.     PRINTED IN U.S.A.

PART NO. 3932439     U

**THIS ENGINE IS EQUIPPED TO REDUCE EXHAUST EMISSIONS**

THE FOLLOWING ADJUSTMENTS ARE NECESSARY TO MAINTAIN THE EFFECTIVENESS OF THE SYSTEM
(With engine at operating temperature, choke open, air cleaner installed, air conditioning off.)
1. Set mixture screw (s) for max. idle rpm and adjust speed screw to obtain **600 RPM IN DRIVE.**
2. Set ignition timing at 4° BTC (Plug vacuum advance line — this step only.)
3. Adjust mixture screw in to obtain a 20 rpm drop (lean roll.)
4. Adjust mixture screw out 1/4 turn.
5. Repeat steps 3 and 4 for second mixture screw (if so equipped.)
6. Readjust speed screw if necessary to specified idle rpm.
See Service Manual for Additional Tune-Up Instruction.     PRINTED IN U.S.A.

PART NO. 3927738     B

**THIS ENGINE IS EQUIPPED TO REDUCE EXHAUST EMISSIONS**

THE FOLLOWING ADJUSTMENTS ARE NECESSARY TO MAINTAIN THE EFFECTIVENESS OF THE SYSTEM
(With engine at operating temperature, choke open, air cleaner installed, air conditioning off.)
1. Set mixture screw(s) for max. idle rpm and adjust speed screw to obtain **700 RPM IN NEUTRAL**
2. Set ignition timing at 4° BTC (plug vacuum advance line — this step only.)
3. Adjust mixture screw in to obtain a 20 rpm drop (lean roll.)
4. Adjust mixture screw out 1/4 turn.
5. Repeat steps 3 and 4 for second mixture screw (if so equipped.)
6. Readjust speed screw if necessary to specified idle rpm.
See Service Manual for Additional Tune-Up Instruction.     PRINTED IN U.S.A

PART NO. 3927744     F

**THIS ENGINE IS EQUIPPED TO REDUCE EXHAUST EMISSIONS**

THE FOLLOWING ADJUSTMENTS ARE NECESSARY TO MAINTAIN THE EFFECTIVENESS OF THE SYSTEM
(With engine at operating temperature, choke open, air cleaner installed, air conditioning on.)
1. Set mixture screw(s) for max. idle rpm and adjust speed screw to obtain **750 RPM IN NEUTRAL.**
2. Set ignition timing at 4° BTC (Plug vacuum advance line — this step only.)
3. Adjust mixture screw in to obtain a 20 rpm drop (lean roll.)
4. Adjust mixture screw out 1/4 turn.
5. Repeat steps 3 and 4 for second mixture screw (if so equipped.)
6. Readjust speed screw if necessary to specified idle rpm.
See Service Manual for Additional Tune-Up Instruction.     PRINTED IN U.S.A

PART NO. 3927748     M

**THIS ENGINE IS EQUIPPED TO REDUCE EXHAUST EMISSIONS**

THE FOLLOWING ADJUSTMENTS ARE NECESSARY TO MAINTAIN THE EFFECTIVENESS OF THE SYSTEM
(With engine at operating temperature, choke open, air cleaner installed, air conditioning on.)
1. Set mixture screw(s) for max. idle rpm and adjust speed screw to obtain **1000 RPM IN NEUTRAL.**
2. Set ignition timing at 12° BTC (Plug vacuum advance line — this step only.)
3. Adjust mixture screw in to obtain a 20 rpm drop (less roll.)
4. Adjust mixture screw out 1/4 turn.
5. Repeat steps 3 and 4 for second mixture screw (if so equipped.)
6. Readjust speed screw if necessary to specified idle rpm.
See Service Manual for Additional Tune-Up Instruction.     PRINTED IN U.S.A

PART NO. 3932459     U

*Emission information labels. All shown are 1968, as follows from top: 300 HP, 350 HP, 300-390-400 HP/Auto, 390 HP/Man, 400-435 HP/Man, 430 HP (L-88). Black on white with red highlight lettering. Shown 46% of actual size.*

**THIS ENGINE IS EQUIPPED TO REDUCE EXHAUST EMISSION**
THE FOLLOWING ADJUSTMENTS ARE NECESSARY TO MAINTAIN SYSTEM EFFECTIVENESS.
(With engine at operating temperature, choke open, air cleaner installed, air conditioning off, parking brake on)
1. Set mixture screws for max. idle rpm and adjust speed screw to specified rpm.
2. Set ignition timing to specification (Plug vacuum advance line – this step only.)
3. Adjust each mixture screw in to obtain a 20 rpm drop, then back out 1/4 turn.
4. If necessary readjust speed screw to specified idle rpm.
IDLE SPECIFICATIONS (See Service Manual for Additional Tune-Up Instructions.)

**CF** — Printed in U.S.A. — PT. NO 3956682

| ENGINE | 255 & 300 HP | 300 HP CORVETTE | 290 HP | 350 & 370HP |
|---|---|---|---|---|
| MAN. TRANS. (IN NEUTRAL) | 700 RPM & 00 TDC | 700 RPM & 4° BTC | 900 RPM & 40 BTC | 750 RPM & 40 BTC |
| AUTO. TRANS. (IN DRIVE) | 600 RPM & 40 BTC | 600 RPM & 40 BTC | NONE | NONE |

---

**THIS ENGINE IS EQUIPPED TO REDUCE EXHAUST EMISSIONS**
THE FOLLOWING ADJUSTMENTS ARE NECESSARY TO MAINTAIN SYSTEM EFFECTIVENESS.
(With engine at operating temperature, choke open, air cleaner installed, air conditioning off, parking brake on)
1. Set mixture screws for max. idle rpm and adjust speed screw to specified rpm.
2. Set ignition timing to specification (Plug vacuum advance line — this step only.)
3. Adjust mixture screw in to obtain a 20 rpm drop, then back out 1/4 turn.
4. If necessary readjust speed screw to specified idle rpm.
IDLE SPECIFICATIONS (See Service Manual for Additional Tune-Up Instructions.)

**CJ** — Printed in U. S. A. — PT. NO. 3959133

| ENGINE | 335, 385 & 390 HP | 400 HP |
|---|---|---|
| MAN. TRANS. (IN NEUTRAL) | 800 RPM & 4° BTC | 750 RPM & 4° BTC |
| AUTO. TRANS. (IN DRIVE) | 600 RPM & 4° BTC | 600 RPM & 4° BTC |

---

**THIS ENGINE IS EQUIPPED TO REDUCE EXHAUST EMISSIONS**
THE FOLLOWING ADJUSTMENTS ARE NECESSARY TO MAINTAIN SYSTEM EFFECTIVENESS
(With engine at operating temperature, choke open, air cleaner installed, air conditioning off, parking brake on)
1. Set mixture screws for max. idle rpm, adjust carb speed screw (Man.) or solenoid screw (Auto.) to specified rpm.
2. Set ignition timing to specification (plug vacuum advance line — this step only).
3. Adjust mixture screw in to obtain a 20 rpm drop, then back out 1/4 turn.
4. If necessary, readjust carb speed screw (Man.) or solenoid screw (Auto.) to specified idle rpm.
IDLE SPECIFICATIONS (See Service Manual for Additional Tune-Up Instructions.)

**CN** — Printed in U.S.A. — PT. NO. 3959136

| ENGINE | 425 & 435 HP | 430 HP |
|---|---|---|
| MAN. TRANS (IN NEUTRAL) | 750 RPM & 4° BTC | 1000 RPM & 12° BTC |
| *AUTO. TRANS (IN DRIVE) | 750 RPM & 4° BTC | 750 RPM & 12° BTC |

*After above adjustment — disconnect solenoid electrically — adjust carburetor speed screw to 500 rpm — reconnect.

---

**VEHICLE EMISSION CONTROL INFORMATION • • • MFD. BY GENERAL MOTORS CORP.**
TUNEUP INSTRUCTIONS: (WITH ENGINE AT OPERATING TEMP., CHOKE OPEN, AIR CLEANER INSTALLED, AIR COND. OFF, PARKING BRAKE ON)
(IF EQUIPPED WITH MIXTURE SCREW CAPS, PERFORM STEP 2 ONLY AND THEN RECONNECT VACUUM LINE).
1. TURN MIXTURE SCREWS IN UNTIL LIGHTLY CONTACTING SEATS, THEN TURN SCREWS BACK OUT FOUR (4) FULL TURNS.
2. DISCONNECT AND PLUG DISTRIBUTOR VACUUM LINE.  SET IGNITION TIMING (WITH RPM AS SPECIFIED IN RED BELOW).
3. READJUST CARBURETOR SPEED SCREW TO OBTAIN 875 RPM (AUTO. IN DRIVE).
4. ADJUST MIXTURE SCREWS EQUALLY TO OBTAIN RECOMMENDED IDLE SPEED (BELOW), RECONNECT VACUUM LINE.
IDLE SPECIFICATION (SEE SERVICE MANUAL FOR ADDITIONAL TUNE-UP INSTRUCTIONS).
ENGINE—350 CU. IN. V8 300 HP.

**CR** — PRINTED IN U.S.A. — PT. NO. 3989372

| | ALL EXCEPT CORVETTE | CORVETTE ONLY |
|---|---|---|
| MANUAL TRANSMISSION (IN NEUTRAL) | 800 RPM & 4° TDC | 800 RPM & 4° BTC; |
| AUTOMATIC TRANSMISSION (IN DRIVE) | 600 RPM & 4° BTC; | 600 RPM & 4° BTC; |

**GM**
THIS VEHICLE CONFORMS TO U.S. DEPT. OF H.E.W. REGULATIONS APPLICABLE TO 1970 MODEL YEAR NEW MOTOR VEHICLES.

---

**VEHICLE EMISSION CONTROL INFORMATION • • • MFD. BY GENERAL MOTORS CORP.**
TUNEUP INSTRUCTIONS: (WITH ENGINE AT OPERATING TEMP., CHOKE OPEN, AIR CLEANER INSTALLED, AIR COND. OFF, PARKING BRAKE ON)
(IF EQUIPPED WITH MIXTURE SCREW CAPS, PERFORM STEP 2 ONLY AND THEN RECONNECT VACUUM LINE).
1. TURN MIXTURE SCREWS IN UNTIL LIGHTLY CONTACTING SEATS, THEN TURN SCREWS BACK OUT FOUR (4) FULL TURNS.
2. DISCONNECT AND PLUG DISTRIBUTOR VACUUM LINE.  SET IGNITION TIMING (WITH RPM AS SPECIFIED IN RED BELOW).
3. READJUST CARBURETOR SPEED SCREW TO OBTAIN 875 RPM (IF MANUAL OR 630 RPM (AUTO. IN DRIVE).
4. ADJUST MIXTURE SCREWS EQUALLY TO OBTAIN RECOMMENDED IDLE SPEED (BELOW), RECONNECT VACUUM LINE.
IDLE SPECIFICATION (SEE SERVICE MANUAL FOR ADDITIONAL TUNE-UP INSTRUCTIONS).
ENGINE—350 CU. IN. V8 350 HP.

**AX** — PRINTED IN U.S.A. — PT. NO. 3980369

| | RPM | TIMING |
|---|---|---|
| MANUAL TRANSMISSION (IN NEUTRAL) | 750 | 8° |
| AUTOMATIC TRANSMISSION (IN DRIVE) | NONE | NONE |

**GM**
THIS VEHICLE CONFORMS TO U.S. DEPT. OF H.E.W. REGULATIONS APPLICABLE TO 1970 MODEL YEAR NEW MOTOR VEHICLES.

*Emission information labels. Top three shown are 1969, lower two are 1970. From top, 300-350 HP, 390-400 HP, 435 & L-88, 300 HP, 350 HP. Black on white with red highlight lettering. Shown 46% of actual size.*

*Emission information labels. Top and top left are 1971, bottom left and top right are 1972, bottom right is 1973. Each label's application is coded at top left of label. Black lettering on white. Shown 24% of actual size.*

*Emission information labels. All shown are 1974 model. Top is for base engine, middle for "454" and bottom for L-82 (incl California). Black lettering on white. Shown 40% of actual size.*

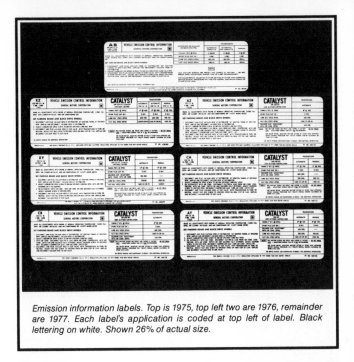

*Emission information labels. Top is 1975, top left two are 1976, remainder are 1977. Each label's application is coded at top left of label. Black lettering on white. Shown 26% of actual size.*

size in 1974, up to the present time. Since 1978 was the silver anniversary of the Corvette, the labels were printed in black on silver, a subtle touch of commemoration. Beginning in 1979, the emissions labels were two piece, about one-and-one-half times the size of 1978. Because of this size, they were placed on the underside of the hood.

## Odd Balls

There are a number of labels which deserve mentioning, but which do not fall into large generalized groups.

A red and white caution label appeared on Corvettes from 1957 through 1972 equipped with positraction. The purpose of the label was to warn that with limited slip differential, "a rear wheel may drive if in contact with ground even though opposite wheel is raised. Do not run engine with vehicle on jack unless transmission is in neutral or park." Since the message was geared to times when the car was jacked, the label was always put where it would be likely seen if the jack was reached for. On '57 through '62 Corvettes, this meant on the spare tire cover. On the later models, it was placed inside the lid of the behind-seat compartment. One style of caution label was probably used for 1957 and 1958 and another style was used between 1959 and 1971. A similar label with subtle wording changes appeared in 1972.

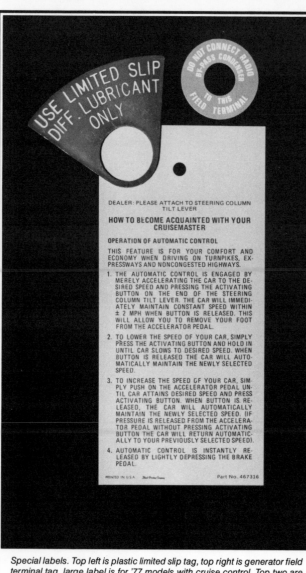

**USE LIMITED SLIP DIFF. LUBRICANT ONLY**

**DO NOT CONNECT RADIO BY-PASS CONDENSER TO THIS FIELD TERMINAL**

DEALER: PLEASE ATTACH TO STEERING COLUMN TILT LEVER

**HOW TO BECOME ACQUAINTED WITH YOUR CRUISEMASTER**

OPERATION OF AUTOMATIC CONTROL

THIS FEATURE IS FOR YOUR COMFORT AND ECONOMY WHEN DRIVING ON TURNPIKES, EXPRESSWAYS AND NONCONGESTED HIGHWAYS.

1. THE AUTOMATIC CONTROL IS ENGAGED BY MERELY ACCELERATING THE CAR TO THE DESIRED SPEED AND PRESSING THE ACTIVATING BUTTON ON THE END OF THE STEERING COLUMN TILT LEVER. THE CAR WILL IMMEDIATELY MAINTAIN CONSTANT SPEED WITHIN ± 2 MPH WHEN BUTTON IS RELEASED. THIS WILL ALLOW YOU TO REMOVE YOUR FOOT FROM THE ACCELERATOR PEDAL.

2. TO LOWER THE SPEED OF YOUR CAR, SIMPLY PRESS THE ACTIVATING BUTTON AND HOLD IN UNTIL CAR SLOWS TO DESIRED SPEED. WHEN BUTTON IS RELEASED THE CAR WILL AUTOMATICALLY MAINTAIN THE NEWLY SELECTED SPEED.

3. TO INCREASE THE SPEED OF YOUR CAR, SIMPLY PUSH ON THE ACCELERATOR PEDAL UNTIL CAR ATTAINS DESIRED SPEED AND PRESS ACTIVATING BUTTON. WHEN BUTTON IS RELEASED, THE CAR WILL AUTOMATICALLY MAINTAIN THE NEWLY SELECTED SPEED. (IF PRESSURE IS RELEASED FROM THE ACCELERATOR PEDAL WITHOUT PRESSING ACTIVATING BUTTON THE CAR WILL RETURN AUTOMATICALLY TO YOUR PREVIOUSLY SELECTED SPEED).

4. AUTOMATIC CONTROL IS INSTANTLY RELEASED BY LIGHTLY DEPRESSING THE BRAKE PEDAL.

PRINTED IN U.S.A.    Part No. 467316

*Special labels. Top left is plastic limited slip tag, top right is generator field terminal tag, large label is for '77 models with cruise control. Top two are white lettering on orange, bottom is black lettering on pale green. Shown 56% of actual size.*

## CAUTION

THIS VEHICLE EQUIPPED WITH LIMITED SLIP DIFFERENTIAL. REAR WHEEL MAY DRIVE IF IN CONTACT WITH GROUND <u>EVEN THOUGH OPPOSITE WHEEL IS RAISED.</u> DO <u>NOT</u> RUN ENGINE WITH VEHICLE ON JACK UNLESS TRANSMISSION IS IN NEUTRAL OR PARK. SEE OWNER'S MANUAL.

PRINTED IN U.S.A.          7-22-58    PART NO. 3745926

*Positraction caution label. This appeared on '57 through '72 Corvettes. Orange lettering on white. Shown 40% of actual size.*

## CAUTION

THIS VEHICLE EQUIPPED WITH HIGH TRACTION DIFFERENTIAL. REAR WHEEL WILL DRIVE IF IN CONTACT WITH GROUND <u>EVEN THOUGH OPPOSITE WHEEL IS RAISED. DO NOT</u> RUN ENGINE WITH VEHICLE ON JACK UNLESS TRANSMISSION IS IN NEUTRAL OR PARK. SEE OWNER'S MANUAL.

PRINTED IN U.S.A.          2-16-71    PART NO. 3998583

*Positraction caution label. This appeared first on '72 model Corvettes. Orange lettering on white. Shown 40% of actual size.*

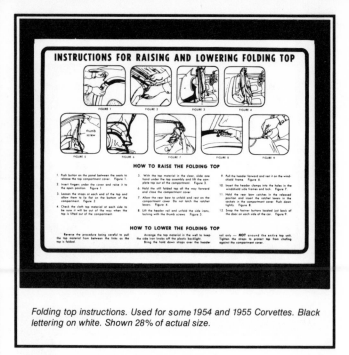

INSTRUCTIONS FOR RAISING AND LOWERING FOLDING TOP

*Folding top instructions. Used for some 1954 and 1955 Corvettes. Black lettering on white. Shown 28% of actual size.*

Though not exactly a label, a red plastic tag with white indented lettering was attached at the filler plug of positraction units. This started with the '65 and continues through current models. The replacement tag says, "USE LIMITED SLIP DIFF. LUBRICANT ONLY." The original said "USE POSITRACTION DIFF. LUBRICANT ONLY."

Another label of interest is a round cardboard tag which spun freely about the field pole of the generator of Corvettes built from 1953 through 1962. It cautioned against connecting the radio by-pass condenser to the field terminal. Use of the tag was terminated in 1963 by the switch to alternators.

Some 1953, 1954, and 1955 model Corvettes had a glass solvent jar for the windshield washer to which was attached a label which read, "Automatic windshield washer—GM accessories—in freezing weather add GM solvent—fill with water to $^3/4$ level."

Later model 1954 and all the 1955 model Corvettes had a large instruction sheet on the inside of the top compartment lid for raising and lowering the folding top. If ever a top needed such instructions, this was it. The label was complete with nine illustrations and twelve raising instructions. Chevrolet deleted the use of the sheet coinciding with the introduction of the '56 model Covette and its much-easier-to-operate top. In the rear of the 1963-67 convertible tops, a paper label was sewn which advised the owner that special care was necessary for the top.

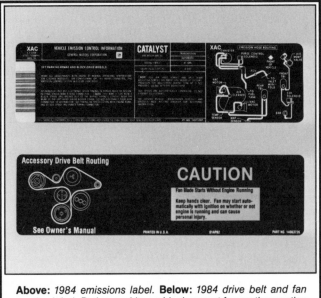

**Above:** *1984 emissions label.* **Below:** *1984 drive belt and fan caution label. Both are white on black except for caution section which is black on yellow. Shown 34% of actual size.*

All 1955, 1956, and hydraulic lifter engines of '58 through '61 had a beautiful little black on metallic gold decal on the oil filler cap. The cap was the breathing type with a mesh insert, and the decal advised washing in kerosene and re-oiling every 3000 miles or "oftener" in severe conditions.

Two labels appeared on or near the steering columns of Corvettes over the years. In 1969, the year the ignition switch moved from the dash to the steering column, a clear label with white lettering was placed on the column and advised "THIS IS A ROTATING INTERLOCK. DO NOT MANIPULATE. DAMAGE MAY RESULT."

The second steering column label was a dealer-installed tag which was hung from the tilt-wheel lever of Corvettes equipped with cruise control. This was a green tag with black printing and contained the expected instructions. It was used only for the 1977 model, the first Corvette to have cruise control available.

The transistor ignition system available (mandatory with the 396, 425hp/427, 435hp/427, L-88, LT-1, LS-6 and LS-7 engines) in Corvettes was identified from 1964 through 1972 with two foil labels. Each was orange and silver with black lettering. One read, "Delco Remy IGNITION COIL FOR TRANSISTOR IGNITION." It was placed on the coil. The second read, "Delco Remy PRIMARY AMPLIFIER FOR MAGNETIC IMPULSE TRANSITOR IGNITION." It was placed on the amplifier.

If a label should get an award for scarcity, surely it would be the fuel warning label for L-88 equipped Corvettes. This label stated, "WARNING: VEHICLE MUST OPERATE ON A FUEL HAVING A MINIMUM OF 103 RESEARCH OCTANE AND 95 MOTOR OCTANE OR ENGINE DAMAGE MAY RESULT." With a twelve and one-half to one compression ratio, it's no wonder these engines needed the best fuel around. The warning label was nothing exotic, just red printing on white vinyl. It was placed on the center console for easy spotting. There were twenty L-88 engine Corvettes built in 1967, eighty in 1968, and 116 in 1969, so the total is a mere 216 cars...and labels.

The LT-1 engine option available from 1970 through 1972 wasn't as rare as the L-88, but it was surely a favorite. It was treated to a special hood decal consisting of stylized letters in outline. Each hood of an LT-1 Corvette received two sets of letters, one set on each side of the hood bulge.

In 1975, the catalytic converter became a Corvette way of life, and burning unleaded fuel became a must. The magic materials in converters don't get along well at all with lead, and using leaded gasoline renders a converter useless after a tank or two. Owners were warned about the fuel requirements in their owner's manuals and on their fuel gauges. Gas tank filler pipes were made smaller to accept only the narrow unleaded pump snouts. And as a final touch, an "UNLEADED FUEL ONLY" sticker was placed on the filler cap cover starting with the '75. There was a white lettered style for dark body colors, and a black lettered style for light body cars. Starting in 1969, carburetors with solenoids had a red and white label that stated "Caution never use to set idle see service manual for adjustments."

The huge clam shell hood of the 1984 Corvette exposed a lot of engine compartment to open view, so designers became concerned that everything, including labels, have an integrated look. Designers picked tones of gray and black for most trim. This was evident in the finishes of the valve covers, new air cleaner, and even the battery top which was redone just for the new Corvette.

The most prominent labels under the hood of the 1984 Corvette are the emissions label and a combination belt routing-fan caution label. Both were placed on the fan shroud during assembly. The belt routing-fan caution label was usually placed on the driver's side and the emissions label on the passenger side. Both read from the rear, and both were white on black except for the fan caution section which was black on yellow.

The belt routing diagram was deemed necessary simply because it was unusual. The fan caution was necessary because the fan was electric and could come on even when the engine was off.

There you have it. Probably everything you ever wanted to know about labels. But if you do want to know more, or if you want to purchase virtually any of the labels discussed in this presentation, the man to contact is Murrell F. Dobbins. Send him a dollar and he'll send you a listing of labels, prices, and applications. Reach him at 624 Kelly Lane, Glenside, Pennsylvania 19038.

# RIVER CITY
# CORVETTE PRINTS

Send _____ prints @ $15.00 (includes mat)   $___.___
Send _____ brushed chrome frames @ $9.95   $___.___
                              Shipping . . . $__**1.00**
              Check/money order enclosed for   $___.___

Mat color desired: ☐ Black   ☐ Green
                   ☐ Grey    ☐ Gold
                   ☐ Blue

Model year desired (specify coupe or convertible):_____

Name_____
Street_____
City_____ State_____ Zip_____

Mail Order To: **Mid America Design**
               **Route 45 North**
               **Effingham, IL 62401**

---

# LABEL INFORMATION

Mr. Dobbins:
Please send Corvette label price and availability
listing. I have enclosed $1.00 for shipping.

Name_____
Street_____
City_____ State_____ Zip_____

Mail Request To: **M. F. Dobbins**
                 **624 Kelly Lane**
                 **Glenside, PA 19038**